Learning to See

Value-Stream Mapping to Create Value and Eliminate Muda

By Mike Rother and John Shook
Foreword by Jim Womack and Dan Jones

A Lean Tool Kit Method and Workbook

THE LEAN ENTERPRISE INSTITUTE
Cambridge, Massachusetts, USA
www.lean.org

Version 1.3
June 2003

With gratitude to family members, Jim Womack, Guy Parsons, OffPiste Design, and our friends at client companies who help us fine tune many ideas.

© Copyright 2003 The Lean Enterprise Institute, Inc.
One Cambridge Center, Cambridge, MA 02142 USA
www.lean.org
Version 1.3, June 2003
ISBN 0-9667843-0-8

Whenever there is a product for a customer,
there is a value stream.
The challenge lies in seeing it.

FOREWORD

By Jim Womack and Dan Jones

When we launched *Lean Thinking* in the Fall of 1996 we urged readers to "Just do it!" in the spirit of Taiichi Ohno and other pioneers of the Toyota system. With more than 300,000 copies in print (including the Second Edition launched in the spring of 2003) and with a steady stream of e-mails, faxes, phone calls, letters, and personal reports from readers telling us of their achievements, we know that many of you are taking our and Ohno's advice.

However, we are also aware that many readers have deviated from the step-by-step transformation process we describe in Chapter 11 of *Lean Thinking* (and enhance in chapter 15 of the Second Edition):

> 1. Find a change agent (how about you?)
>
> 2. Find a sensei (a teacher whose learning curve you can borrow)
>
> 3. Seize (or create) a crisis to motivate action across your firm

But then they have jumped to Step Five:

> 5. Pick something important and get started removing waste quickly, to surprise yourself with how much you can accomplish in a very short period.

Yet the overlooked Step Four is actually the most critical:

> 4. Map the entire value stream for all of your product families

Unfortunately, we find that many readers have ignored our advice to conduct this critical step before diving into the task of waste elimination. Instead in too many cases we find companies rushing headlong into massive muda elimination activities — kaizen offensives or continuous improvement blitzes. These well intentioned exercises fix one small part of the value stream for each product and value does flow more smoothly through that course of the stream. But then the value flow comes to a halt in the swamp of inventories and detours ahead of the next downstream step. The net result is no cost savings reaching the bottom line, no service and quality improvements for the customer, no benefits for the supplier, limited sustainability as the wasteful norms of the whole value stream close in around the island of pure value, and frustration all around.

Typically the kaizen offensive with its disappointing results becomes another abandoned program, soon to be followed by a "bottleneck elimination" offensive (based on the Theory of Constraints) or a Six Sigma initiative (aimed at the most visible quality problems facing a firm), or … But these produce the same result: Isolated victories over muda, some of them quite dramatic, which fail to improve the whole.

Therefore, as the first "tool kit" project of the Lean Enterprise Institute, we felt an urgent need to provide lean thinkers the most important tool they will need to make sustainable progress in the war against muda: the value-stream map. In the pages ahead Mike Rother and John Shook explain how to create a map for each of your value streams and show how this map can teach you, your managers, engineers, production associates, schedulers, suppliers, and customers to see value, to differentiate value from waste, and to get rid of the waste.

Kaizen efforts, or any lean manufacturing technique, are most effective when applied strategically within the context of building a lean value stream. The value-stream map permits you to identify every process in the flow, pull them out from the background clutter of the organization, and build an entire value stream according to lean principles. It is a tool you should use every time you make changes within a value stream.

As in all of our tool kit projects, we have called on a team with a wide variety of practical and research experience. Mike Rother studies Toyota, has worked with many manufacturers to introduce lean production flows, and teaches at the University of Michigan. John Shook spent over ten years with the Toyota Motor Corporation, much of it teaching suppliers to *see*, and is now a Senior Advisor to the Lean Enterprise Institute. Together they possess a formidable body of knowledge and experience — a painfully constructed learning curve — which they are now sharing with you.

We hope readers of *Lean Thinking* and participants in the activities of the Lean Enterprise Institute will use the mapping tool immediately and widely. And we hope you will tell us how to improve it! Because our own march toward perfection never ends, we need to hear about your successes and, even more important, about the nature of your difficulties.

So again, "Just do it!" but now at the level of the value stream, product family by product family — beginning inside your company and then expanding beyond. Then tell us about your experience so we can share your achievements with the entire lean network.

Jim Womack & Dan Jones
Brookline, Massachusetts, USA
and Ross-on-Wye, Herefordshire, UK
June 2003

CONTENTS

INTRODUCTION

We have discovered an amazing thing. While so many of us have been scratching our heads trying to figure out why the road to lean has been rockier than it should be, a vital yet simple tool that can help us make real progress toward becoming lean has been right under our noses.

One of us, Mike, had long searched for a means to tie together lean concepts and techniques, which seemed more disparate than they should be, as he worked on many plant floor implementation efforts. Mike noticed the mapping method while studying Toyota's lean implementation practices. He realized mapping had potential far beyond its usual usage, formalized the tool, and built a training method around it that has proved extraordinarily successful.

The other of us, John, has known about the "tool" for over ten years, but never thought of it as important in its own right. As John worked with Toyota, mapping was almost an afterthought—a simple means of communication used by individuals who learn their craft through hands-on experience.

At Toyota, the method—called "Value-Stream Mapping" in this workbook — is known as "Material and Information Flow Mapping." It isn't used as a training method, or as a means to "Learn to See." It is used by Toyota Production System practitioners to depict current and future, or "ideal" states in the process of developing implementation plans to install lean systems. At Toyota, while the phrase "value stream" is rarely heard, infinite attention is given to establishing flow, eliminating waste, and adding value. Toyota people learn about three flows in manufacturing: the flows of material, information, and people/process. The Value-Stream Mapping method presented here covers the first two of these flows, and is based on the Material and Information Flow Maps used by Toyota.

Like many others in recent years, we were struggling to find ways to help manufacturers think of flow instead of discrete production processes and to implement lean systems instead of isolated process improvements. We struggled to help manufacturers make lasting, systematic improvements that would not only remove wastes, but also the sources of the wastes so that they would never come back. For those who simply give the mapping tool a try, we have been pleased to see how exceptionally effective the tool has proved to be in focusing attention on flow and helping them to *see*. Now we present it to you.

Mike Rother and John Shook
Ann Arbor, Michigan
May 1998

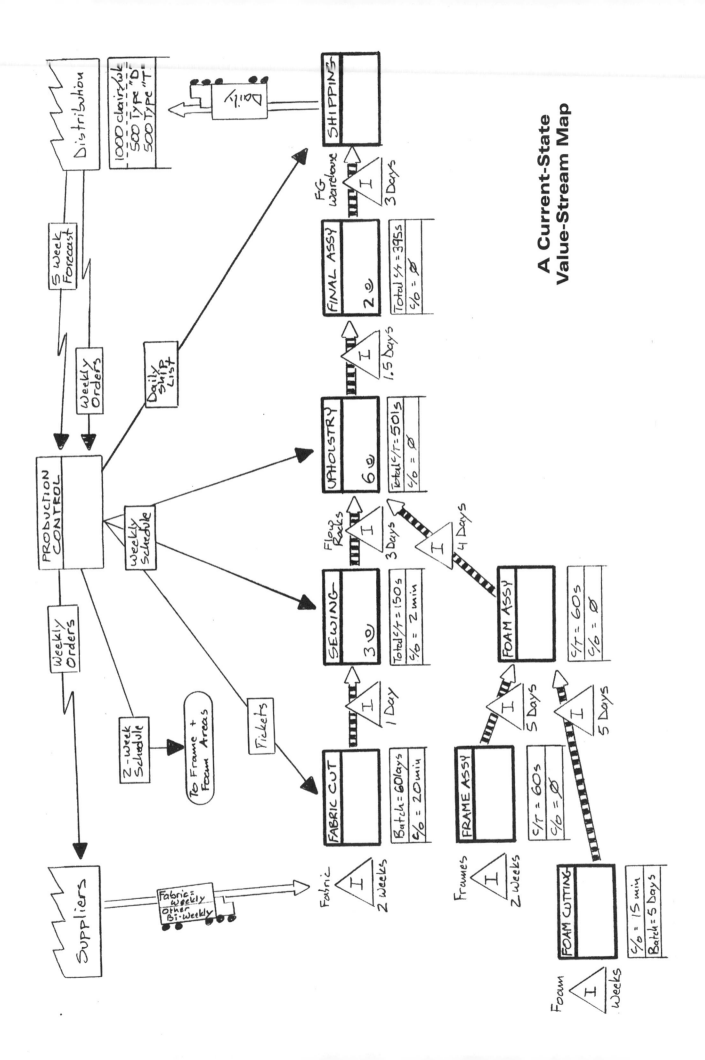

A Current-State
Value-Stream Map

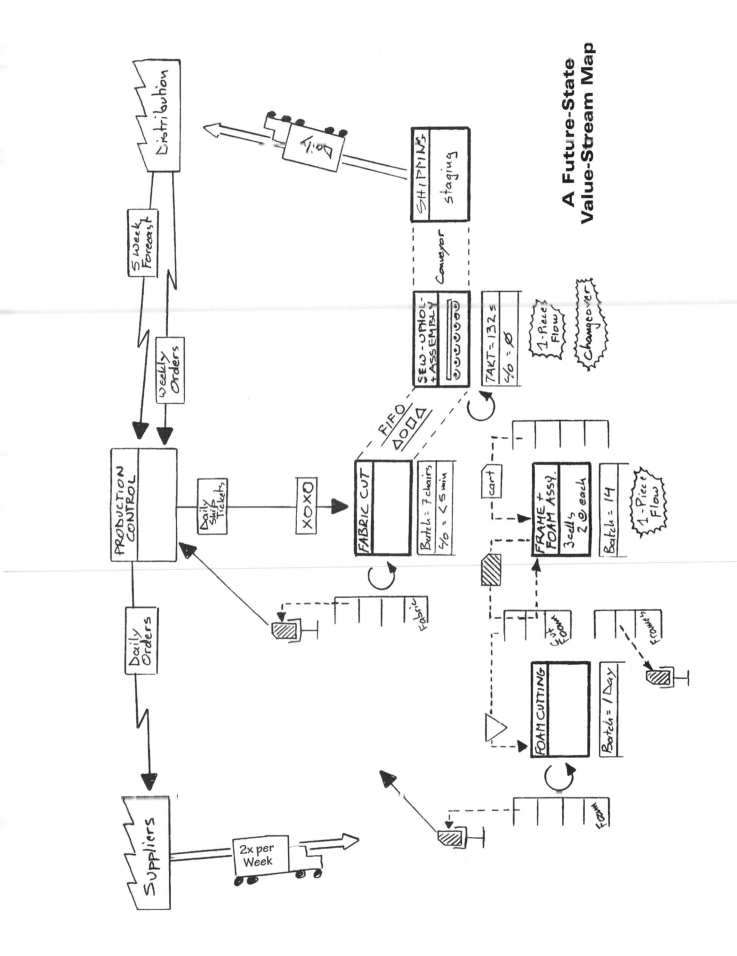

A Future-State Value-Stream Map

PART I: GETTING STARTED

- **What is Value-Stream Mapping**

- **Material and Information Flow**

- **Selecting a Product Family**

- **The Value-Stream Manager**

- **Using the Mapping Tool**

START HERE

PART I: GETTING STARTED

- **What is Value-Stream Mapping**

- **Material and Information Flow**

- **Selecting a Product Family**

- **The Value-Stream Manager**

- **Using the Mapping Tool**

What is Value-Stream Mapping

"Value stream" may be a new phrase in your vocabulary. A value stream is all the actions (both value added and non-value added) currently required to bring a product through the main flows essential to every product: (1) the production flow from raw material into the arms of the customer, and (2) the design flow from concept to launch. This workbook looks at the production flow from customer demand back through raw material, which is the flow we usually relate to lean manufacturing and precisely the area where many have struggled to implement lean methods.

Taking a value stream perspective means working on the big picture, not just individual processes, and improving the whole, not just optimizing the parts. If you truly look at the whole and go all the way from molecules into the arms of the customer, you will need to follow the value stream for a product across many firms and even more facilities. But mapping this entire stream is too much for getting started!

This workbook covers the "door-to-door" production flow inside a plant, including shipment to the plant's customer and delivery of supplied parts and material, where you can design a future-state vision and start implementing it right away. This is a good level at which to begin your mapping and lean implementation effort.

As your lean experience and confidence grow you can expand outward, from the plant level toward the complete molecules-to-end-user map. Note, however, that in large companies when a product's value stream passes through more than one of your own facilities, expanding the mapping effort to include the flow through your other facilities should happen very quickly.

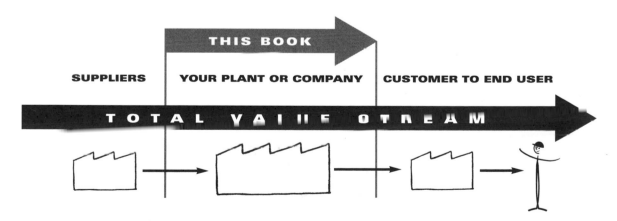

Value-stream mapping is a pencil and paper tool that helps you to see and understand the flow of material and information as a product makes its way through the value stream. What we mean by value-stream mapping is simple: Follow a product's production path from customer to supplier, and carefully draw a visual representation of every process in the material and information flow. Then ask a set of key questions and draw a "future-state" map of how value should flow.

Doing this over and over is the simplest way — and the best way we know — to teach yourself and your colleagues how to see value and, especially, the sources of waste.

WHY VALUE-STREAM MAPPING IS AN ESSENTIAL TOOL

- It helps you visualize more than just the single-process level, i.e. assembly, welding, etc., in production. You can see the flow.

- It helps you see more than waste. Mapping helps you see the sources of waste in your value stream.

- It provides a common language for talking about manufacturing processes.

- It makes decisions about the flow apparent, so you can discuss them. Otherwise, many details and decisions on your shop floor just happen by default.

- It ties together lean concepts and techniques, which helps you avoid "cherry picking".

- It forms the basis of an implementation plan. By helping you design how the whole door-to-door flow should operate — a missing piece in so many lean efforts — value-stream maps become a blueprint for lean implementation. Imagine trying to build a house without a blueprint!

- It shows the linkage between the information flow and the material flow. No other tool does this.

- It is much more useful than quantitative tools and layout diagrams that produce a tally of non-value-added steps, lead time, distance traveled, the amount of inventory, and so on. Value-stream mapping is a qualitative tool by which you describe in detail how your facility should operate in order to create flow. Numbers are good for creating a sense of urgency or as before/after measures. Value-stream mapping is good for describing what you are actually going to do to affect those numbers.

Practice drawing value-stream maps and you will learn to see your shop floor in a way that supports lean manufacturing. Just remember that the point of getting lean is not "mapping," which is just a technique. What's important is implementing a value-adding flow. To create this flow you need a "vision" of the flow. Mapping helps you see and focus on flow with a vision of an ideal, or at least improved, state.

You shouldn't run out and map all your value streams right away. To benefit from value-stream mapping you should make use of it on the shop floor, mapping a value stream you will actually be implementing. If you are planning changes in a value stream, be sure to draw a future-state map first. If you are designing a new production process, first map a future state for the value stream. Considering a new scheduling system? Draw the future state first. Changing production managers? Use value-stream maps to help ensure an effective hand-off and continued implementation progress.

Material and Information Flows

Within the production flow, the movement of material through the factory is the flow that usually comes to mind. But there is another flow — of information — that tells each process what to make or do next. Material and information flow are two sides of the same coin. You must map both of them.

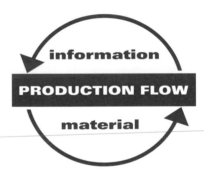

In lean manufacturing the information flow is treated with just as much importance as the material flow. Toyota and its suppliers may use the same basic material-conversion processes as mass producers, like stamping/welding/assembly, but Toyota plants regulate their production quite differently from mass producers. The question to ask yourself is, "How can we flow information so that one process will make only what the next process needs when it needs it?"

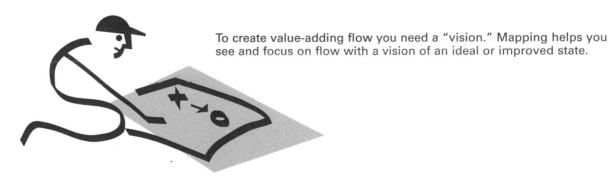

To create value-adding flow you need a "vision." Mapping helps you see and focus on flow with a vision of an ideal or improved state.

Selecting a Product Family

One point to understand clearly before starting is the need to focus on one product family. Your customers care about their specific products, not all your products. So you will not be mapping everything that goes through the shop floor. Unless you have a small, one-product plant, drawing all your product flows on one map is too complicated. Value-stream mapping means walking and drawing the processing steps (material and information) for one product family from door to door in your plant.

Identify your product families from the customer end of the value stream. A family is a group of products that pass through similar processing steps and over common equipment in your downstream processes. In general, you should not try to discern product families by looking at upstream fabrication steps, which may serve many product families in a batch mode. Write down clearly what your selected product family is, how many different finished part numbers there are in the family, how much is wanted by the customer, and how often.

Note:

If your product mix is complicated you can create a matrix with assembly steps and equipment on one axis, and your products on the other axis (see below).

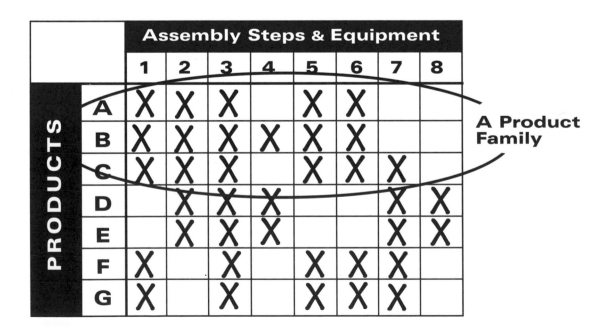

	Assembly Steps & Equipment							
PRODUCTS	1	2	3	4	5	6	7	8
A	X	X	X		X	X		
B	X	X	X	X	X	X		
C	X	X	X		X	X	X	
D		X	X	X			X	X
E		X	X	X			X	X
F	X		X		X	X	X	
G	X		X		X	X	X	

A Product Family

The Value-Stream Manager

You may have already noticed that tracing the value stream for a product family will take you across organizational boundaries in your company. Because companies tend to be organized by departments and functions, instead of by the flow of value-creating steps for product families, you often find that — surprise — no one is responsible for the value-stream perspective. (It's no wonder we have focused too heavily on process-level kaizen!) It is astoundingly rare to visit a facility and find one person who knows the entire material and information flow for a product (all processes and how each is scheduled). Yet without this, parts of the flow will be left to chance—meaning that individual processing areas will operate in a way that is optimum from their perspective, not the value-stream's perspective.

To get away from the isolated islands of functionality you need one person with lead responsibility for understanding a product family's value stream and improving it. We call this person a Value-Stream Manager, and suggest that in this capacity they report to the top person at your site. This way they will have the power necessary to help change happen.

Who is responsible for the Value Stream?

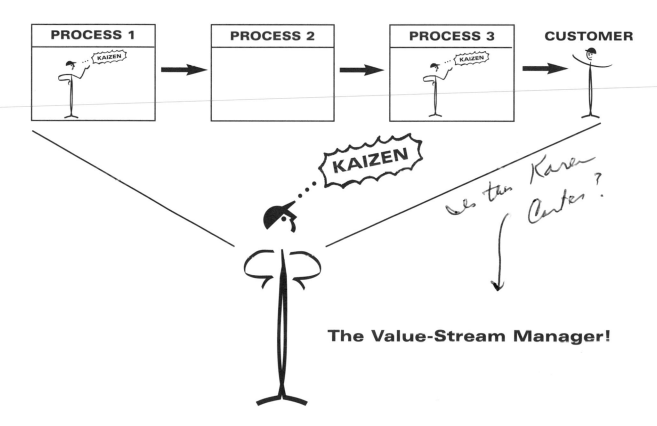

The Value-Stream Manager!

Many people get involved in lean implementation, and all need an understanding of value-stream mapping and the ability to read a future-state map. But the mapping and future-state implementation team needs to be led by someone who can see across the boundaries over which a product's value-stream flows and make change happen there. Value-stream improvement — "flow kaizen" — is management doing kaizen.

Do not make the mistake of splitting up the mapping task among area managers and then hope to stitch together their individual segments. Likewise, don't map your organization. Map the flow of products through your organization.

two kinds of kaizen

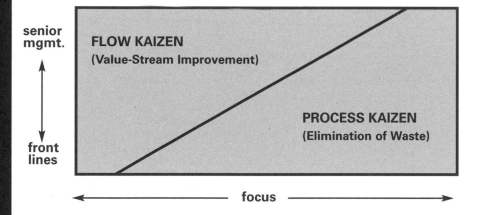

Note:

Both flow kaizen (value-stream improvement) and process-level kaizen (elimination of waste at the shop floor team level) are necessary in your company; improvement in one improves the other. Flow kaizen focuses on material and information flow (which require a high vantage point to see) and process kaizen focuses on people and process flow.

Using the Mapping Tool

Value-stream mapping can be a communication tool, a business planning tool, and a tool to manage your change process. Value-stream mapping is essentially a language and, as with any new language, the best way to learn mapping is to practice it formally at first, until you can use it instinctively.

Value-stream mapping initially follows the steps shown at right. Notice that "Future-State Drawing" is highlighted, because your goal is to design and introduce a lean value stream. A current state without a future state is not much use. The future-state map is most important.

The first step is drawing the current state, which is done by gathering information on the shop floor. This provides the information you need to develop a future state. Notice that the arrows between current and future state go both ways, indicating that development of the current and future states are overlapping efforts. Future-state ideas will come up as you are mapping the current state. Likewise, drawing your future state will often point out important current-state information you have overlooked.

The final step is to prepare and begin actively using an implementation plan that describes, on one page, how you plan to achieve the future state. Then, as your future state becomes reality, a new future-state map should be drawn. That's continuous improvement at the value-stream level. There must always be a future-state map.

The beauty of this bureaucracy- and Powerpoint-free method is that your mapping and implementation team ends up with only a few sheets of paper (the future state and a plan to achieve it) that can transform your business!

Note:

Value-stream mapping for one product family should not take too much time. In about two days you should have a future-state map drawn to the point where implementation can begin. Don't get hung up trying to make all the details on your future-state map perfectly correct. Fine-tune your future-state map as implementation progresses.

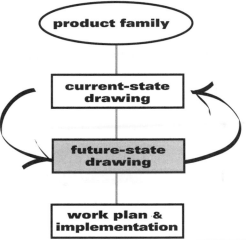

Initial Value-Stream
Mapping Steps

SUMMARY - YOUR STARTING POINT

• Select a product family

• Have one person personally lead the mapping effort

• Begin at the "door-to-door" level

• Consider both the material and information flows

PART II: THE CURRENT-STATE MAP

- Drawing the Current-State Map
- Your Turn

PART II: THE CURRENT-STATE MAP

PURPOSE: MAKE CLEAR THE CURRENT PRODUCTION SITUATION BY DRAWING THE MATERIAL AND INFORMATION FLOWS.

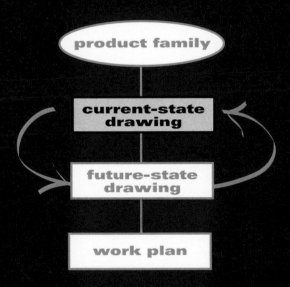

Drawing the Current-State Map

Developing a future state begins with an analysis of the current production situation. This section shows you how to create a "current-state map" using a simple example factory we call Acme Stamping. Mapping begins at the level of the door-to-door flow in your plant, where you draw process categories like "assembly" or "welding," instead of recording each processing step.

We use a set of symbols, or "icons," summarized inside the back cover of this workbook, to represent processes and flows. You can develop additional icons of your own, but keep them consistent within your company so that everyone will know how to draw and understand the maps that you need to institute lean manufacturing.

Once you see the overall flow through the plant, you can change the level of magnification; zooming in to map every individual step within a process category, or zooming out to encompass the value stream external to your plant.

levels of mapping the value stream for a product family

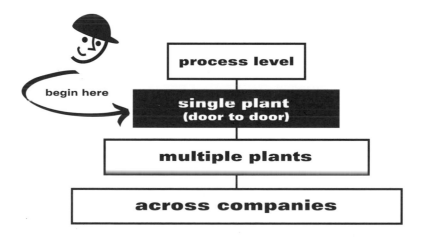

A few mapping tips:

- **Always collect current-state information while walking along the actual pathways of material and information flows yourself.**

- **Begin with a quick walk along the entire door-to-door value stream,** to get a sense of the flow and sequence of processes. After the quick walk through, go back and gather information at each process.

- **Begin at the shipping end and work upstream,** instead of starting at the receiving dock and walking downstream. This way you will begin with the processes that are linked most directly to the customer, which should set the pace for other processes further upstream.

- **Bring your stopwatch and do not rely on standard times or information that you do not personally obtain.** Numbers in a file rarely reflect current reality. File data may reflect times when everything was running well, for example the first-time-this-year three-minute-die-change, or the once-since-the-plant-opened week when no expediting was necessary. Your ability to envision a future state depends upon personally going to where the action is and understanding and timing what is happening. (Possible exceptions to this rule are data on machine uptime, scrap/rework rates, and changeover times.)

- **Map the whole value stream yourself,** even if several people are involved. Understanding the whole flow is what value-stream mapping is about. If different people map different segments, then no one will understand the whole.

- **Always draw by hand in pencil.** Begin your rough sketch right on the shop floor as you conduct your current-state analysis, and clean it up later—again by hand and in pencil. Resist the temptation to use a computer.

Always draw by hand in pencil.

Drawing by hand can be done without delay, while you are on the floor. As you draw you will think of further information that you need.

Drawing by hand means that you can do it yourself, which is key to understanding the material and information flows.

Drawing by hand means you will focus on understanding the flow, instead of on how to use the computer. The point of value-stream mapping is not the map, but understanding the flow of information and material.

Having to manually fine-tune your drawings will improve your mapping ability. Keep an eraser handy!

Drawing the Current-State Map

To get started, fold out the Acme Stamping data set inside the back cover of this workbook and refer to it as we build Acme's current-state map. Also get yourself a blank sheet of paper (11" x 17" ledger size paper — called "A3" in Europe and Japan — works well for us) and a pencil so you can draw along with us.

Acme's product family to be mapped is a stamped-steel steering bracket. This component holds the steering column to the body of a car and is produced in two versions: one for left-hand-side drive cars, the other for right-hand-side drive. Because there is no variability in the design beyond the left-drive and right-drive versions, the product family is very narrow in this example.

The boundaries of Acme's first map are the door-to-door flow of the product through Acme's plant, including basic supplied material (coil steel) and the shipment of completed brackets to Acme's customer, the State Street Automotive Assembly plant. Mapping starts with the customer requirements. We'll represent the customer's assembly plant with a **factory** icon, placed in the upper right-hand portion of the map. Underneath this icon we'll draw a **data box** recording the requirements of Acme's assembly plant customer.

FACTORY

DATA BOX

Note:

As noted in *Lean Thinking*, the critical place to begin any improvement effort is clear specification of the value of a product as perceived by the end customer. Otherwise you run the risk of improving a value stream which efficiently provides the end customer with something other than what's really wanted. Thus mapping begins with the customer requirements.

State Street Assembly operates on two shifts. This customer uses 18,400 steering brackets per month and requires daily shipments. Typically 12,000 "left-hand drive" brackets and 6,400 "right-hand drive" are needed every month. State Street Assembly requests palletized returnable tray packaging with 20 brackets in a tray and up to 10 trays on a pallet. The customer orders in multiples of trays, so the "pack size" is one tray of 20 parts. All of the brackets on each pallet need to be either left-drive or right-drive style.

```
┌─────────────────────┐
│   State Street      │
│   Assembly          │
└─────────────────────┘
┌─────────────────────┐
│ 18,400 pcs/mo       │
│  –12,000 "L"        │
│  – 6,400 "R"        │
├─────────────────────┤
│ Tray = 20 pieces    │
├─────────────────────┤
│ 2 Shifts            │
└─────────────────────┘
```

First View of the Current-State Map
Showing the Customer

ASSEMBLY

The next mapping step is to draw the basic production processes. To indicate a process we use a **process box**. The general rule of thumb for the door-to-door map is that a process box indicates a process in which the material is flowing. Since drawing one box for every single processing step would make the map unwieldy, we use the process box to indicate one area of material flow, ideally a continuous flow. The process box stops wherever processes are disconnected and the material flow stops.

For example, an assembly process with several connected workstations, even if there is some WIP inventory between stations, would be drawn as one process box. But if one assembly process is disconnected from the next assembly process downstream, with inventory stagnating, accumulating, and being moved in batches between them, then two process boxes would be used.

Likewise, a machining line of say 15 sequential machining operations, such as drilling, tapping, etc., that are connected by a transfer line between each operation would be shown with only one process box on the door-to-door map, even if some inventory accumulates between machines. (If a detailed process-level map is later made for the machining area alone, then you would draw one box for every individual machining step.) But if there are distinctly separate machining processes in the plant, with inventory between them stagnating and transferred in batches, then each gets its own process box.

Material flow is drawn from left to right on the bottom half of the map in the order of processing steps; not according to the physical layout of the plant. At Acme Stamping we find six processes in the steering bracket material flow, which occur in the following order:

- Stamping
- Spot-Welding Workstation 1
- Spot-Welding Workstation 2
- Assembly Workstation 1
- Assembly Workstation 2
- Shipping

Each of Acme's spot-welding and assembly workstations are separate processes because, as you can see in the overhead view of the plant (inside the back cover of this workbook), products do not move in a flow from one to the next. Inventory is moved in baskets and stagnates between the workstations. On the map, each of these processes is represented by a process box, from left to right on the bottom half of the page.

Note:

Unlike the Acme Stamping example, many value streams have multiple flows that merge. Draw such flows over one another as shown here. But don't try to draw every branch if there are too many. Choose the key components first, and get the others later if you need to.

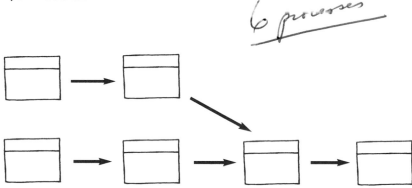

6 processes

As you walk this flow on the shop floor, you need to collect data that is important for deciding what the future state will be. So a data box is drawn under each process box. After mapping several current and future states you will know instinctively what process information you need. The list at right will help you get started.

At Acme Stamping, we have the following information to record in the data box under each processing step: the **cycle time** (time that elapses between one part coming off the process to the next part coming off, in seconds); the **changeover time** to switch from producing one product type to another (in this case switching between left-drive and right-drive brackets); the **number of people**

To help you get started here is a list of typical process data:

✔ C/T (cycle time)

✔ C/O (changeover time)

✔ uptime (on-demand machine uptime)

✔ EPE (production batch sizes)

✔ number of operators

✔ number of product variations

✔ pack size

✔ working time (minus breaks)

✔ scrap rate

required to operate the process (which can be indicated with an operator icon as shown inside the process boxes); the **available working time** per shift at that process (in seconds, minus break, meeting, and cleanup times); and machine **uptime** information.

In the "stamping" data box we also show **EPEx**, which stands for "every part every _____" and is a measure of production batch size. For example, if you change over to produce a particular part once every three days, then the production batch size is about three days worth of parts. Notice that the cycle time is the time between parts coming off the end of the process and not the total cycle time it takes one part to move through all process steps. Also notice that available work time divided by cycle time multiplied by uptime percent is a measure of current process capacity, if no changeovers are made.

Note:

Value-stream mapping uses seconds as the time unit for cycle times, takt times, and available working times. Many of you have been taught to use decimal minutes to measure time, but that unit is unnecessarily complicated. Value-stream mapping is a tool everyone should be able to use.

3150 pieces
2 days

As you walk the product's material flow you will find places where inventory accumulates. These points are important to draw on the current-state map because they tell you where the flow is stopping. We use a "warning triangle" icon to capture the location and amount of **inventory**. (If the inventory accumulates in more than one location between two processes, draw a triangle for each location.)

Some Lean Measurements

Cycle Time

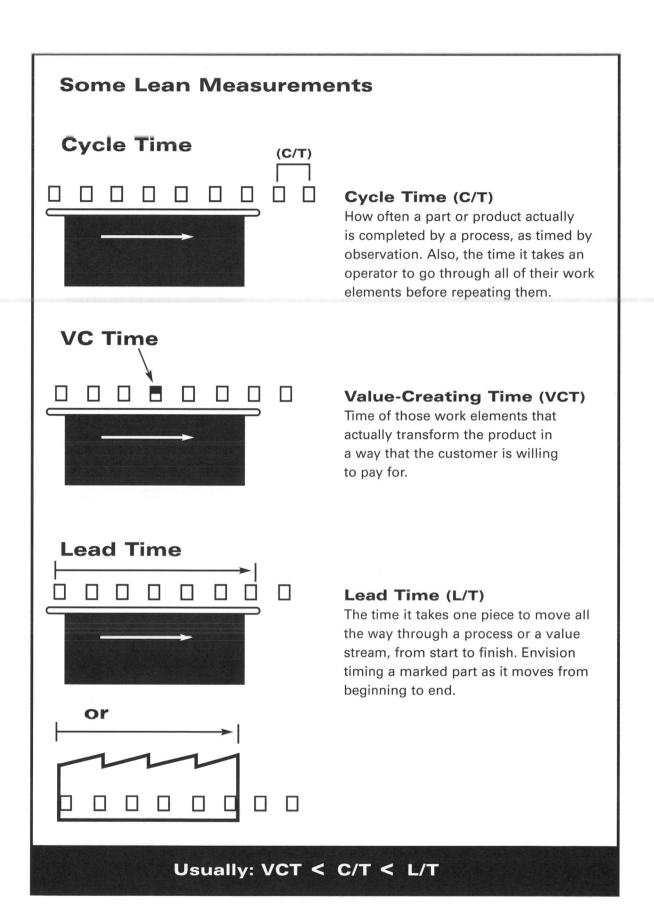

(C/T)

Cycle Time (C/T)
How often a part or product actually is completed by a process, as timed by observation. Also, the time it takes an operator to go through all of their work elements before repeating them.

VC Time

Value-Creating Time (VCT)
Time of those work elements that actually transform the product in a way that the customer is willing to pay for.

Lead Time

Lead Time (L/T)
The time it takes one piece to move all the way through a process or a value stream, from start to finish. Envision timing a marked part as it moves from beginning to end.

or

Usually: VCT < C/T < L/T

At Acme Stamping there is raw material inventory, finished goods inventory, and inventory between each process. The observed amount of inventory is recorded below the triangles, in quantity and/or time.

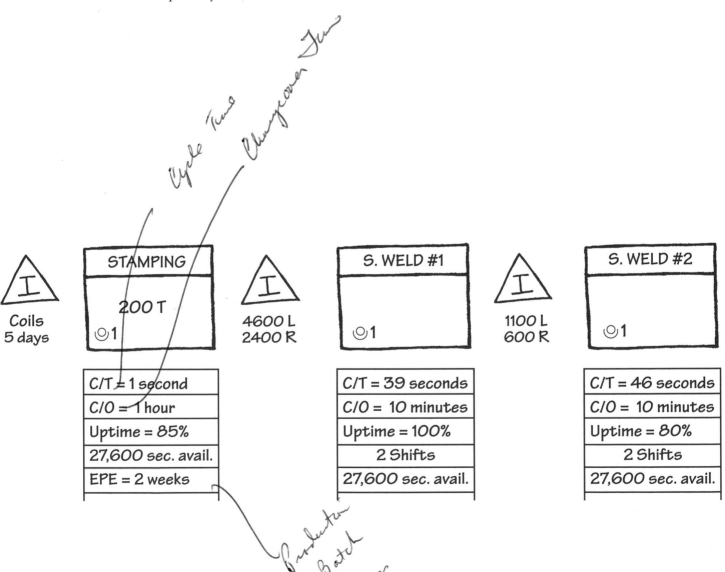

| Coils 5 days | | STAMPING | | 200 T | ⊙1 | | 4600 L 2400 R | | S. WELD #1 | ⊙1 | | 1100 L 600 R | | S. WELD #2 | ⊙1 |

STAMPING	S. WELD #1	S. WELD #2
C/T = 1 second	C/T = 39 seconds	C/T = 46 seconds
C/O = 1 hour	C/O = 10 minutes	C/O = 10 minutes
Uptime = 85%	Uptime = 100%	Uptime = 80%
27,600 sec. avail.	2 Shifts	2 Shifts
EPE = 2 weeks	27,600 sec. avail.	27,600 sec. avail.

Second View of the Current-State Map with all Processes, Data Boxes, and Inventory Triangles

State Street Assembly

18,400 pcs/mo
−12,000 "L"
− 6,400 "R"
Tray = 20 pieces
2 Shifts

1600 L
850 R

ASSEMBLY #1
 1

C/T = 62 seconds
C/O = Ø
Uptime = 100%
2 Shifts
27,600 sec. avail.

1200 L
640 R

ASSEMBLY #2
1

C/T = 40 seconds
C/O = Ø
Uptime = 100%
2 Shifts
27,600 sec. avail.

2700 L
1440 R

SHIPPING
Staging

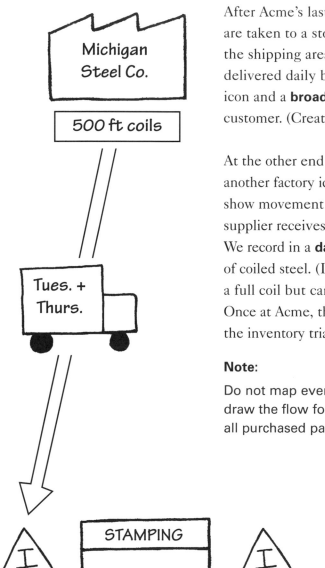

Michigan
Steel Co.

500 ft coils

Tues. +
Thurs.

After Acme's last assembly workstation, steering brackets in trays are taken to a storage area (triangle icon). They are then staged in the shipping area according to the daily shipping schedule and delivered daily by truck to the customer's assembly plant. A **truck** icon and a **broad arrow** indicate movement of finished goods to the customer. (Create rail or air freight icons if you need them.)

At the other end of the map, we'll represent the steel supplier with another factory icon. We use the same truck icon and broad arrow to show movement of material from the supplier to Acme. The steel supplier receives a weekly order from Acme and ships twice a week. We record in a **data box** that the supplier's pack size is a 500 foot roll of coiled steel. (In other words, the supplier cannot deliver less than a full coil but can deliver any number of full coils, as requested.) Once at Acme, the coil steel is taken to a storage area, as shown by the inventory triangle.

Note:

Do not map every purchased part in your product family. Just draw the flow for one or two main raw materials. Presentation of all purchased parts is best shown on a process-level layout diagram.

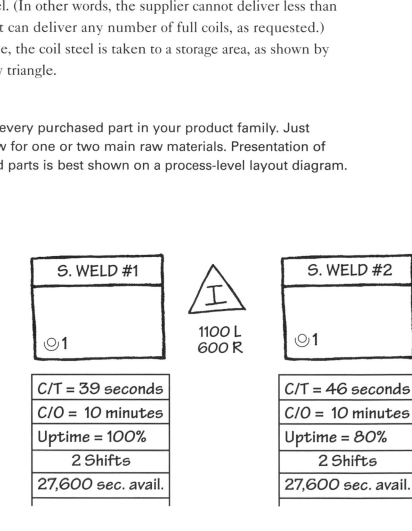

Coils
5 days

STAMPING
200 T
⊚1

C/T = 1 second
C/O = 1 hour
Uptime = 85%
27,600 sec. avail.
EPE = 2 weeks

4600 L
2400 R

S. WELD #1
⊚1

C/T = 39 seconds
C/O = 10 minutes
Uptime = 100%
2 Shifts
27,600 sec. avail.

1100 L
600 R

S. WELD #2
⊚1

C/T = 46 seconds
C/O = 10 minutes
Uptime = 80%
2 Shifts
27,600 sec. avail.

State Street Assembly

| 18,400 pcs/mo |
| −12,000 "L" |
| − 6,400 "R" |
| Tray = 20 pieces |
| 2 Shifts |

Third View of the Current-State Map Showing the Material Flow

1x Daily

| I | **ASSEMBLY #1** | I | **ASSEMBLY #2** | I | **SHIPPING** |

| 1600 L | ⊙1 | 1200 L | ⊙1 | 2700 L | Staging |
| 850 R | | 640 R | | 1440 R | |

C/T = 62 seconds		C/T = 40 seconds
C/O = Ø		C/O = Ø
Uptime = 100%		Uptime = 100%
2 Shifts		2 Shifts
27,600 sec. avail.		27,600 sec. avail.

information flow

electronic
information flow

But how does the Acme plant, each process within the plant, and the steel coil supplier know how much to make and when? Let's add the second aspect of our value-stream map: **the information flow**. To do this we'll need a few more icons and arrows, in particular a **narrow line** to show information flows. This line is modified with a lightening -like wiggle when the information flows electronically (via electronic data interchange) rather than by paper. A **small box** icon or node is used to label or describe different information-flow arrows.

Information flow is drawn from right to left in the top half of the map space. In our Acme Stamping example, we draw the flow of information back from the State Street Assembly Plant to Acme's Production Control department and from there to Acme's steel-coil supplier. Notice there are separate lines for the forecasts and daily orders, as these are different information flows.

The Acme production control department is drawn with a **process box**, including the note that Acme uses a computerized Materials Requirements Planning system (MRP) to schedule the shop floor. Acme production control collects information from customers and the shop floor, consolidates and processes it, and sends specific instructions to each manufacturing process about what it should produce and when. Production control also sends a daily shipping schedule to the shipping department.

Note

In your shop floor mapping efforts you may find information flows more complicated than at Acme Stamping. For example, in many shops supervisors count inventory and make schedule adjustments based on such information. (We call this "go see" scheduling and show it with an eyeglass icon.) Try to incorporate these "informal" scheduling processes into your map using the same information arrows and nodes. If it looks messy, that's probably because it is!

"go see"
scheduling

As you figure out how each process knows what to make for its customer (the following process) and when to make it, you can identify a critical piece of mapping information: material movements that are pushed by the producer, not pulled by the customer. "Push" means that a process produces something regardless of the actual needs of the downstream customer process and "pushes" it ahead.

Push typically results from producing to a schedule that guesses what the next process will need. Unfortunately this is nearly impossible to do consistently because schedules change and production rarely goes exactly according to schedule. When each process has its own schedule it is operating as an "isolated island," disconnected from any sort of downstream customer. Each process is able to set batch sizes and to produce at a pace that make sense from its perspective, instead of the value-stream's perspective.

In this situation, the supplying processes will tend to make parts their customer processes don't need now, and those parts are pushed into storage. This type of "batch and push" processing makes it almost impossible to establish the smooth flow of work from one process to the next that is a hallmark of lean production.

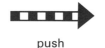

push

The mapping icon for **push movement** of material is a striped arrow. At Acme Stamping, only the shipping department is connected in any way to a "customer." Each of the other processes is producing according to a schedule, so the transfer of material from one process to the next is occurring via push. A push arrow is drawn between each process.

Note

Be wary of material movements that someone calls "pull," but are actually still a form of "push." (See page 46 for a discussion of supermarket pull systems.) To qualify as pull, parts <u>must not</u> be produced or conveyed when there is no kanban, and the quantity of parts produced <u>must be</u> the same as specified on the kanban. "Go see" schedule adjustments are not a true pull.

GO LOOK!

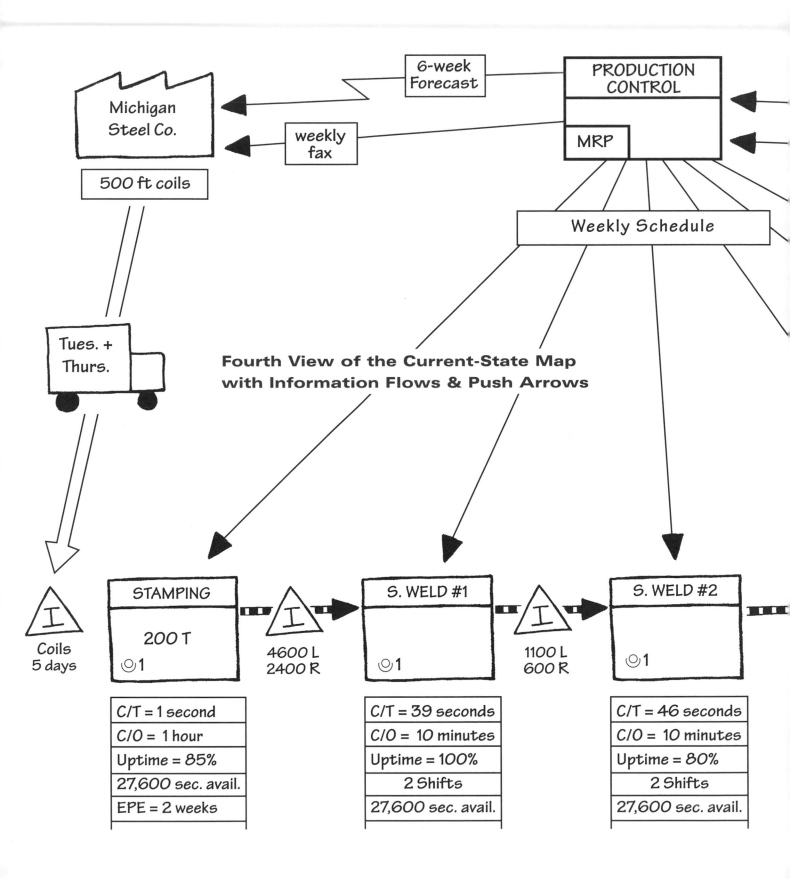

**Fourth View of the Current-State Map
with Information Flows & Push Arrows**

6-week
Forecast

PRODUCTION
CONTROL

MRP

weekly
fax

Michigan
Steel Co.

500 ft coils

Weekly Schedule

Tues. +
Thurs.

Coils
5 days

STAMPING		S. WELD #1		S. WELD #2
200 T	4600 L 2400 R	1	1100 L 600 R	1
1				

C/T = 1 second	C/T = 39 seconds	C/T = 46 seconds
C/O = 1 hour	C/O = 10 minutes	C/O = 10 minutes
Uptime = 85%	Uptime = 100%	Uptime = 80%
27,600 sec. avail.	2 Shifts	2 Shifts
EPE = 2 weeks	27,600 sec. avail.	27,600 sec. avail.

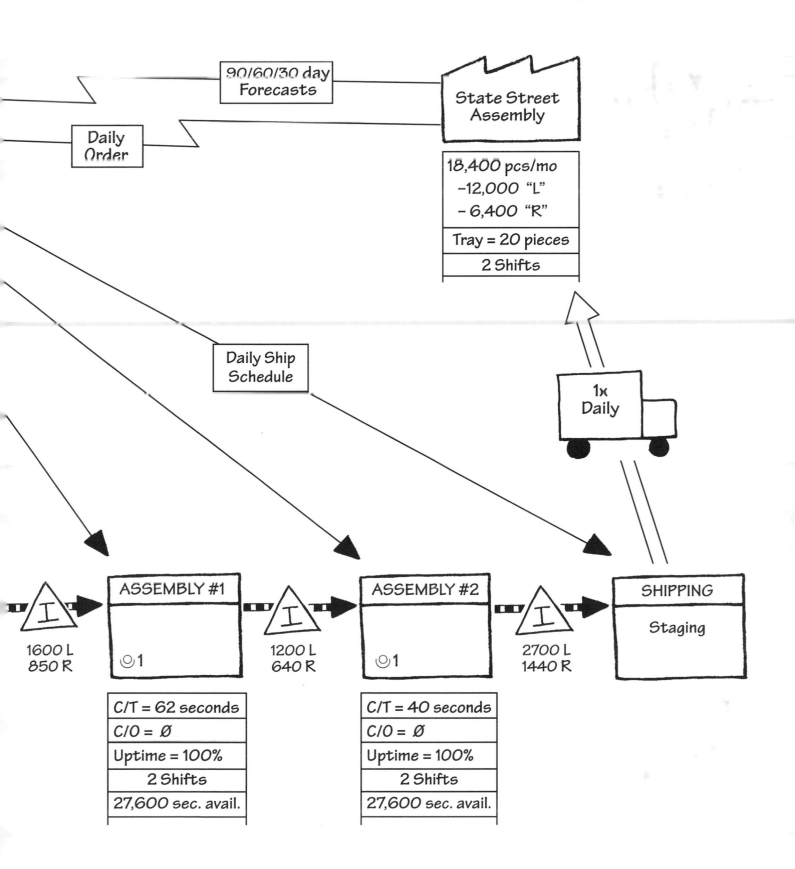

90/60/30 day
Forecasts

Daily
Order

State Street
Assembly

| 18,400 pcs/mo |
| –12,000 "L" |
| – 6,400 "R" |
| Tray = 20 pieces |
| 2 Shifts |

Daily Ship
Schedule

1x
Daily

| I | ASSEMBLY #1 | I | ASSEMBLY #2 | I | SHIPPING |

1600 L
850 R

◎1

1200 L
640 R

◎1

2700 L
1440 R

Staging

| C/T = 62 seconds |
| C/O = Ø |
| Uptime = 100% |
| 2 Shifts |
| 27,600 sec. avail. |

| C/T = 40 seconds |
| C/O = Ø |
| Uptime = 100% |
| 2 Shifts |
| 27,600 sec. avail. |

In looking at the almost completed map you can now see the basic pattern of all value-stream maps, specifically a flow of physical product from left to right across the lower portion of the map and a flow of information about this product from right to left across the upper portion. You can also see how a value-stream map differs from the typical visual tool used in operations analysis — the facility layout. The value-stream map makes the welter of events shown in the plant layout suddenly comprehensible from the perspective of a product's value stream and its customer.

With the data from observation of current operations drawn or recorded on the map, we can summarize the current condition of this value stream. Draw a **timeline** under the process boxes and inventory triangles to compile the production lead time, which is the time it takes one part to make its way through the shop floor, beginning with arrival as raw material through to shipment to the customer.

timeline

Note

The shorter your production lead time, the shorter the time between paying for raw material and getting paid for product made from those materials. A shorter production lead time will lead to an increase in the number of inventory turns, a measure with which you may be more familiar.

Lead times (in days) for each inventory triangle are calculated as follows: inventory quantity divided by the daily customer requirement. By adding the lead times through each process and through each inventory triangle in the material flow, we can arrive at a good estimate of total production lead time. At Acme Stamping this number is 23.6 days. (For maps with multiple upstream flows, use the longest time path to compute total lead time.)

Now add up only the value-adding times or the processing times, for each process in the value stream. Comparing value-added or processing time to total lead time should give you quite a shock. At Acme Stamping the total processing time involved in making one piece is only 188 seconds, whereas that piece takes 23.6 days to make its way through the plant.

Note:

At Acme Stamping the lead time through a process and the cycle time are the same. In many cases however, the lead time for one part to move through a process is longer than the cycle time. You can draw both lead time through a process and the value-adding time as follows:

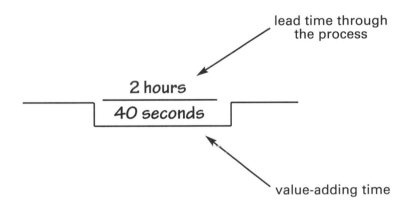

Completed Current-State Map with Lead-Time Bars & Data

GO LOOK!

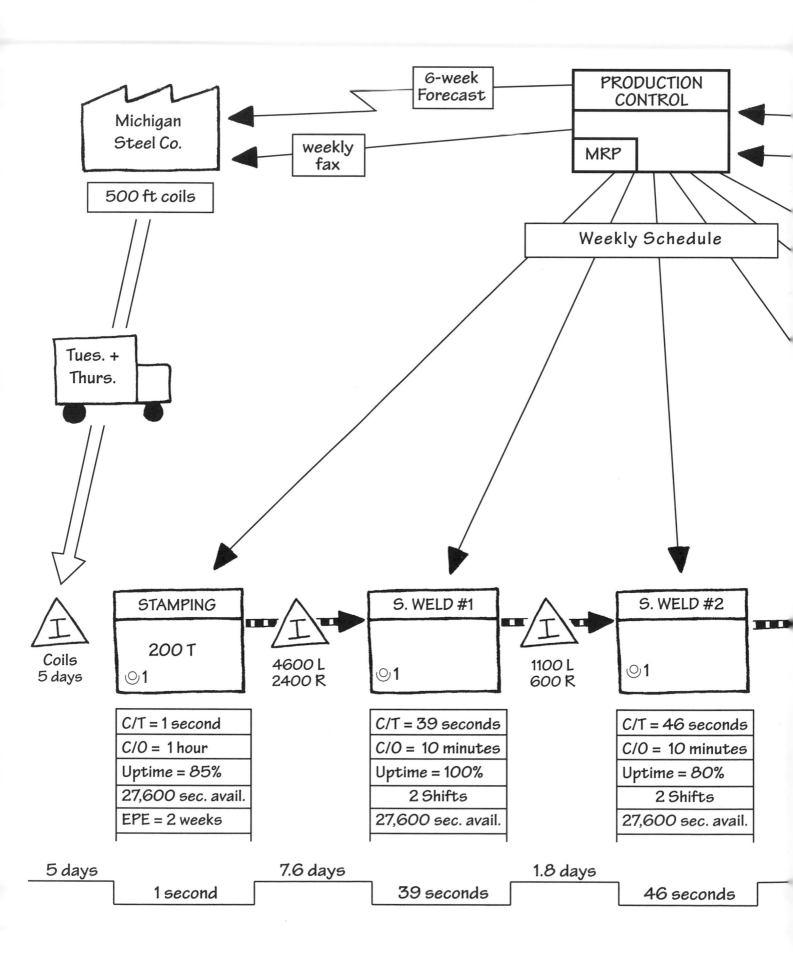

6-week Forecast

PRODUCTION CONTROL

MRP

Michigan Steel Co.

weekly fax

500 ft coils

Weekly Schedule

Tues. + Thurs.

Coils
5 days

STAMPING

200 T

◎ 1

| C/T = 1 second |
| C/O = 1 hour |
| Uptime = 85% |
| 27,600 sec. avail. |
| EPE = 2 weeks |

4600 L
2400 R

S. WELD #1

◎ 1

| C/T = 39 seconds |
| C/O = 10 minutes |
| Uptime = 100% |
| 2 Shifts |
| 27,600 sec. avail. |

1100 L
600 R

S. WELD #2

◎ 1

| C/T = 46 seconds |
| C/O = 10 minutes |
| Uptime = 80% |
| 2 Shifts |
| 27,600 sec. avail. |

5 days

1 second

7.6 days

39 seconds

1.8 days

46 seconds

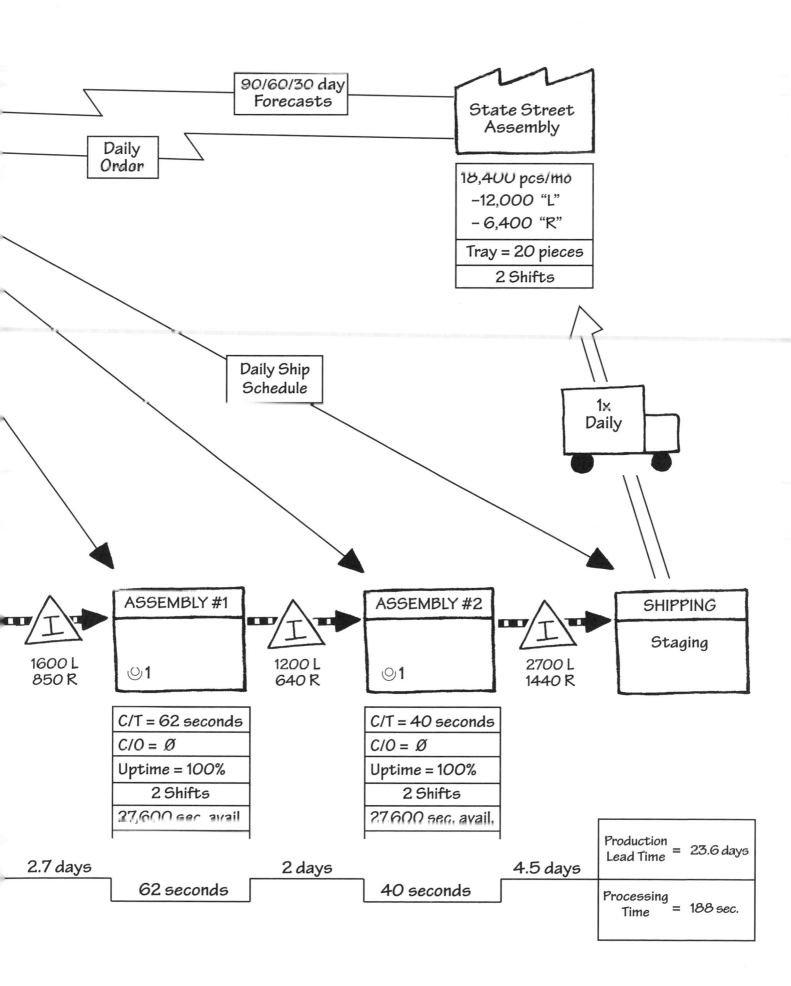

What have we accomplished so far?

We hope that now you can see the value stream and begin to recognize areas of overproduction. However, a "current-state map" and the effort required to create it are pure muda unless you use your map to quickly create and implement a "future-state map" that eliminates sources of waste and increases value for the customer. We will describe just how to do this in the rest of *Learning to See*.

Your Turn

Before we proceed to the creation of a "future-state map", you may find it useful to get a little more "current-state" practice. We therefore have provided the following current-state facts for a more custom-products oriented company called "TWI Industries." We invite you now to take another blank sheet of 11" x 17" paper and carefully draw a current-state value-stream map for TWI Industries. You can then compare your current-state map with the one we've drawn for TWI, as shown in Appendix B. (However, be sure not to peek at Appendix C!)

Value-Stream Mapping Data Set

TWI Industries

TWI Industries produces several components for tractors. This case concerns one product family—Steering Arms—which are produced in many configurations. TWI's customers for this product family are both original-equipment tractor builders and the aftermarket repair business.

Because of the wide variety of product configurations and the fact that customer configuration requirements vary from order to order, steering arms are a "make-to-order" business. It currently takes a customer order 27 days to get through TWI's production processes. This long lead time and a significant order backlog have prompted TWI to quote a 60-day lead time to customers. However, TWI's customers cannot accurately predict their size requirements more than 2 weeks out, and thus they make adjustments to their orders 2 weeks before shipment. These order adjustments lead to order expediting on the shop floor at TWI.

Although TWI Production Control releases customer orders to production roughly in the order that they are received, orders are batched by product configuration on the shop floor to reduce the number of time-consuming changeovers. This also creates a need for order expediting.

The Product

- A steering arm is a metal rod with a forged fitting welded to each end.
- TWI's steering arms are available in 20 different lengths, 2 diameters, and with 3 different types of end fittings. (Each end of the steering arm can have a different fitting.) This means there are 240 different steering arm part numbers that TWI supplies.

Customer Requirements

- 24,000 pieces per month.
- A customer order ranges from 25 to 200 pieces, with an average of 50 pieces.
- Corrugated-box packaging with up to 5 steering arms in a box.
- Several daily shipments per day by truck to various customers.
- Each customer's configuration requirements vary greatly from order to order.
- TWI requires orders to arrive 60 days before shipping date.
- Customers often adjust their size mix 2 weeks before the shipping date.

Production Processes (see diagram)

- TWI's processes for the steering arm product family involve cutting a metal rod followed by welding end fittings to the rod, deflash (machine removal of excess weldment), painting at an outside vendor, and subsequent assembly of the end fittings. The forged end-fitting sockets are also machined at TWI. Finished steering arms are staged and shipped to customers on a daily basis.
- Switching between rod lengths requires a 15 minute changeover at the cutting, welding, and deflash operations.
- Switching between rod diameters takes a 1 hour changeover at the cutting, welding, and deflash operations. The longer change-over for diameters is due mostly to an increased quality-control inspection requirement.
- Switching between the three types of forged end fittings takes a 2 hour changeover at the machining operation.
- Steel rods are supplied by Michigan Steel Co. The lead time for obtaining rods is 16 weeks. There are two shipments per month.
- Raw forgings for the end fittings are supplied by Indiana Castings. The lead time for obtaining forgings is 12 weeks. There are two shipments per month.

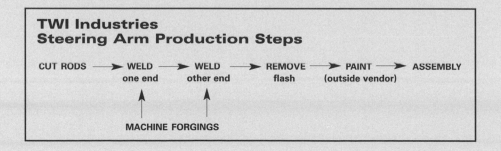

Work Time

- 20 days in a month.
- Two shift operation in all production departments.
- Eight (8) hours every shift, with overtime if necessary.
- Two 15-minute breaks during each shift.
  Manual processes stop during breaks.
  Unpaid lunch.

TWI Production Control Department

- Receives customer orders 60 days out and and enters them to MRP.
- Generates one "shop order" per customer, which follows the order through the entire production process.
- Releases shop orders to production 6 weeks before shipment to accelerate MRP's procurement of rods and forgings.
- Issues daily "priority" list to production supervisors. Supervisors sequence shop orders through their departments according to this list.
- Receives customer size-changes 2 weeks before shipment and advises supervisors to expedite these orders.
- Issues daily shipping schedule to Shipping Department.

Process Information

1. Cutting (The saw cuts rods for many TWI products)

- Manual process with 1 operator.
- Cycle Time: 15 seconds.
- Changeover time: 15 minutes (for length) and 1 hour (for diameter).
- Reliability: 100%.
- Observed Inventory.
    - 20 days of uncut rods before the saw.
    - 5 days of cut rod.

2. Welding Workstation I (dedicated to this product family)

- This operation welds the first machined forging to the rod.
- Automatic process, with operator load & unload external to machine cycle.
- Cycle Time: Operator = 10 seconds, Machine = 30 seconds.
- Changeover time: 15 minutes (for length) and 1 hour (for diameter).
- Reliability: 90%.
- Observed Inventory: 3 days of welded arms.

3. Welding Workstation II (dedicated to this product family)
- This operation welds the second machined forging to the rod.
- Automatic process, with operator load & unload external to machine cycle.
- Cycle Time: Operator = 10 seconds, Machine = 30 seconds.
- Changeover time: 15 minutes (for length) and 1 hour (for diameter).
- Reliability: 80%.
- Observed Inventory: 3 days of welded arms.

4. Deflash Workstation (dedicated to this product family)
- Automatic process, with operator load & unload external to machine cycle.
- Cycle Time: Operator = 10 seconds, Machine = 30 seconds.
- Changeover time: 15 minutes (for length) and 1 hour (for diameter).
- Reliability: 100%.
- Observed Inventory: 5 days of deflashed arms.

5. Painting (steering arms are shipped to an outside vendor for painting)
- Painting lead time = 2 days.
- One daily truck pickup of unpainted arms and drop-off of painted arms.
- Observed Inventory: 2 days at the painter 6 days of painted arms at TWI.

6. End-fitting Assembly (dedicated to this product family)
- Manual process with six operators.
- Total Work Time Per Piece: 195 seconds.
- Changeover time: 10-minute fixture swap.
- Reliability: 100%.
- Observed Finished-Goods Inventory in Warehouse:
    - 4 days of finished steering arms.

7. Machining of Forgings (dedicated to this product family)
- Automatic machining process with one machine attendant
- Cycle Time: 30 seconds.
- Changeover time: 2 hours.
- Reliability: 100%.
- Observed Inventory:
    - 20 days of raw forgings from the supplier.
    - 4 days of machined forgings.

8. Shipping Department
- Removes parts from finished goods warehouse and stages them for truck shipment to customer.

PART III: WHAT MAKES A VALUE STREAM LEAN?

- Overproduction

- Characteristics of a
  Lean Value Stream

PART III: WHAT MAKES A VALUE STREAM LEAN?

- **Overproduction**

- **Characteristics of a Lean Value Stream**

What Makes a Value Stream Lean?

The Catch-22 of designing your future-state value stream is that you will be much more successful if you've already done it many times! This is where a sensei who has experienced the learning curve that you need can be a big help.

However, we don't all have access to a good sensei and some of you don't want one anyway. After all, Ohno didn't have consultants guiding him as he built Toyota's production system through trial and error after World War II. In fact, it is an invaluable learning experience to take a crack at a future-state value stream with your own resources, even if you soon see problems with your approach and modify it in the spirit of continuous improvement. And, until a day in the future when you can make your products in a complete continuous flow with lead time short enough to allow production only to confirmed order and zero changeover times between products, you will require a number of future-state maps (no matter how much help you get from a sensei), each a little leaner and closer to that ideal.

But you shouldn't start from scratch either. The manufacturing world has now had lots of experience with lean manufacturing, so you can begin with established principles and practices and work to adapt them to future states for your own value streams.

Before we show you how to draw a future-state map (Part IV), let's summarize some of the most important lean principles to help you get started.

Overproduction

We can see the fundamental problems with mass (or "batch-and-push") production in the Acme Stamping current state: each process in the value stream operates as an isolated island, producing and pushing product forward according to schedules it receives from Production Control instead of the actual needs of the downstream "customer" process. Since this material output is not yet needed, it must be handled, counted, stored, and so on — pure muda. Defects remain hidden in the inventory queues until the downstream process finally uses the parts and discovers the problem (which is by then extensive and hard to trace). As a result, while the value-creating time for producing one product is very short, the total time that product spends getting through the plant is very long.

To reduce that overly long lead time from raw material to finished good you need to do more than just try to eliminate obvious waste. Too many lean implementation efforts have been "seven-waste" scavenger hunts. While it is good to be aware of waste, your future-state designs need to eliminate the sources, or "root causes" of waste in the value stream. Once the problems of mass production can be seen in a way that reveals these root causes, your company can work at finding original solutions.

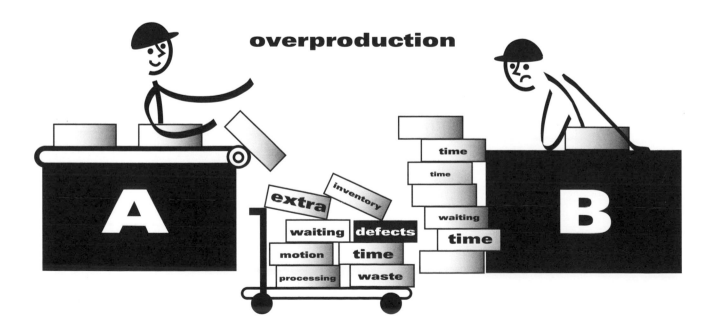

The most significant source of waste is overproduction, which means producing more, sooner or faster than is required by the next process. Overproduction causes all kinds of waste, not just excess inventory and money tied up in that inventory. Batches of parts must be stored, requiring storage space; handled, requiring people and equipment; sorted; and reworked. Overproduction results in shortages, because processes are busy making the wrong things. It means that you need extra operators and equipment capacity, because you are using some of your labor and equipment to produce parts that are not yet needed. It also lengthens the lead time, which impairs your flexibility to respond to customer requirements.

The constant attention Toyota puts on avoiding overproduction is what most clearly distinguishes their value streams from mass production value streams. Mass production thinking says that the more and faster you produce, the cheaper it is to produce. But this is true only from a direct-cost-per-item perspective as measured by traditional accounting practices, and ignores all the other very real costs associated with overproduction and the wastes it causes.

Characteristics of a Lean Value Stream

All we are really trying to do in lean manufacturing is to get one process to make only what the next process needs when it needs it. We are trying to link all processes—from the final consumer back to raw material—in a smooth flow without detours that generates the shortest lead time, highest quality, and lowest cost.

So how can you—on your shop floor—actually get one process to produce only what the next process needs when it needs it? Fortunately you can follow Toyota's lead and use the guidelines on the following pages.

All we are really trying to do in lean manufacturing is to get one process to make only what the next process needs when it needs it. We are trying to link all processes — from the final consumer back to raw material — in a smooth flow without detours that generates the shortest lead time, highest quality, and lowest cost.

takt time
Synchronizes pace of production to match pace of sales

$$\text{takt time} = \frac{\text{available working time per day}}{\text{customer demand rate per day}}$$

$$\text{example:} \quad \frac{27,600 \text{ sec.}}{460 \text{ pieces}} = \textbf{60 seconds}$$

Guideline #1: Produce to your takt time.

"Takt time" is how often you should produce one part or product, based on the rate of sales, to meet customer requirements. Takt time is calculated by dividing the customer demand rate per day (in units), into your available working time per day (in seconds).

Takt time is used to synchronize the pace of production with the pace of sales, particularly at the "pacemaker process" (see p. 49). It is a reference number that gives you a sense for the rate at which a process should be producing. It helps you see how you are doing and what you need to improve. On the future-state map, takt times are noted in the data boxes.

Producing to takt sounds simple, but it requires concentrated effort to:
- provide fast response (within takt) to problems
- eliminate causes of unplanned downtime
- eliminate changeover time in downstream, assembly-type processes

Note

In some industries, such as distribution, custom products, and process industries, it can take some creativity to define "units" of customer demand. One solution is to define a "unit" as how much work can be done at your bottleneck process in a "takt" of say, 10 minutes. Then break your orders up into units of this takt interval.

Guideline #2: Develop continuous flow wherever possible.

Continuous flow refers to producing one piece at a time, with each item passed immediately from one process step to the next without stagnation (and many other wastes) in between. Continuous flow is the most efficient way to produce, and you should use a lot of creativity in trying to achieve it.

The mapping icon we use to indicate continuous flow is simply the process box. In your future-state drawing, each process box should describe an area of flow. So if you introduce more continuous flow in your future state, then two or more current-state process boxes would combine into one box on the future-state map.

Sometimes you'll want to limit the extent of a pure continuous flow, because connecting processes in a continuous flow also merges all their lead times and down times. A good approach can be to begin with a combination of continuous flow and some pull/FIFO. Then extend the range of continuous flow as process reliability is improved, changeover times are reduced to near zero, and smaller, in-line equipment is developed.

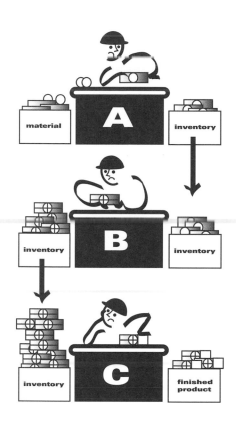

isolated islands

continuous flow

Guideline #3: Use supermarkets to control production where continuous flow does not extend upstream.

There are often spots in the value stream where continuous flow is not possible and batching is necessary. There can be several reasons for this including:

- Some processes are designed to operate at very fast or slow cycle times and need to change over to serve multiple product families (e.g. stamping or injection molding.)
- Some processes, such as those at suppliers, are far away and shipping one piece at a time is not realistic.
- Some processes have too much lead time or are too unreliable to couple directly to other processes in a continuous flow.

Resist the temptation to schedule these processes via an independent scheduling function, because a schedule is only an estimate of what the next process will actually need. Instead, control their production by linking them to their downstream customers, most often via supermarket-based pull systems. Simply put, you usually need to install a pull system where continuous flow is interrupted and the upstream process must still operate in a batch mode.

supermarket pull system

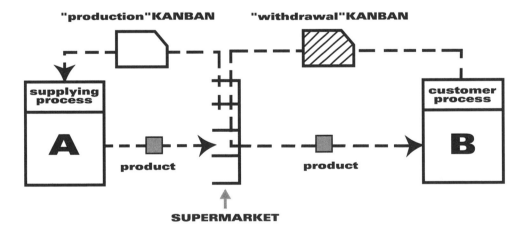

① **CUSTOMER PROCESS** goes to supermarket and withdraws what it needs when it needs it.

② **SUPPLYING PROCESS** produces to replenish what was withdrawn

PURPOSE: Controls production at supplying process without trying to schedule. Controls production between flows

Note:

A "production" kanban triggers production of parts, while a "withdrawal" kanban is a shopping list that instructs the material handler to get and transfer parts.

The purpose of placing a pull system between two processes is to have a means of giving accurate production instruction to the upstream process, without trying to predict downstream demand and scheduling the upstream process. Pull is a method for controlling production between flows. Get rid of those elements of your MRP that try to schedule the different areas of your plant. Let the downstream process' withdrawals out of a supermarket determine what the upstream process produces when and in which quantity.

There are several icons associated with a supermarket pull system:

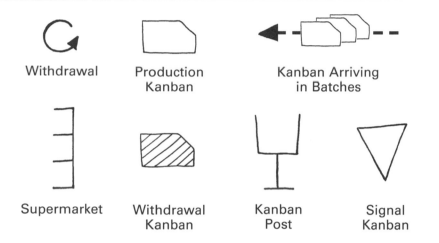

| Withdrawal | Production Kanban | Kanban Arriving in Batches |

| Supermarket | Withdrawal Kanban | Kanban Post | Signal Kanban |

The supermarket icon is open on the left side, which faces the supplying process. This is because this supermarket belongs to the supplying process and is used to schedule that process. On the factory floor, supermarkets should ordinarily be located near the supplying process to help that process maintain a visual sense of customer usage and requirements. The "customer" process material handler then comes to the supplier's supermarket and withdraws what is needed. These withdrawals trigger the movement of pre-printed kanban (typically cards) from the supermarket to the supplier process, where they are used as the only production instruction for that process.

Before you decide to use any supermarket pull systems, be sure that you have introduced continuous flow across as many process steps as is possible. You don't want supermarkets of inventory, and the extra material handling requirements, between processes unless you must.

There is another icon similar to the supermarket icon, but closed on all sides. This icon represents "safety stock," which is used as a hedge against problems such as downtime, or "buffer stock," which is used to protect you against sudden fluctuations in customer orders. Safety stock should be temporary — used only until the root cause of a problem is found and eliminated. To ensure that safety stock does not instead become a permanent crutch, there should be strict rules for being able to use it and it may even be kept under lock and key. Typically this means getting permission from a high-level manager, who will want to see a root-cause problem analysis and countermeasure plan before giving permission!

Note:

Pull systems are a nice way to control production between processes that cannot be tied together in a continuous flow, but sometimes it is not practical to keep an inventory of all possible part variations in a pull-system supermarket. Examples include custom parts (where each part produced is unique), parts that have a short shelf life, and costly parts that are used infrequently.

max. 20 pieces

$-FIFO\rightarrow$

- In some of these cases you can use a FIFO ("first in, first out") lane between two decoupled processes to substitute for a supermarket and maintain a flow between them. Think of a FIFO lane like a chute that can hold only a certain amount of inventory, with the supplying process at the chute entrance and the customer process at the exit. If the FIFO lane gets full, the supplying process must stop producing until the customer has used up some of the inventory.

  For example, you ship to an outside plating process one time per day. The plater can only handle 50 pieces per day, so you set up a FIFO lane sized to hold at most 50 pieces of plating work. Whenever the lane is full the upstream process stops producing parts to be plated. In this manner, the FIFO lane prevents the supplying process from overproducing, even though the supplying process is not linked to the plater via continuous flow or a supermarket. When a FIFO lane is full no additional kanban are released to the upstream process. (Note that some people refer to the FIFO approach as "CONWIP".)

sequenced-
pull ball

- Sometimes you can install a "sequenced pull" between two processes, instead of a complete supermarket that has all components represented in it. Sequenced pull means that the supplying process produces a predetermined quantity (often one subassembly) directly to the customer process' order. This works if lead time in the supplying process is short enough for production to order, and if the customer process follows strict "ordering" rules. Sequenced pull is sometimes called the "golf ball system" because colored balls or disks (that roll nicely down a chute to the supplying process) are sometimes used to provide production instruction.

an example of a "FIFO Lane"

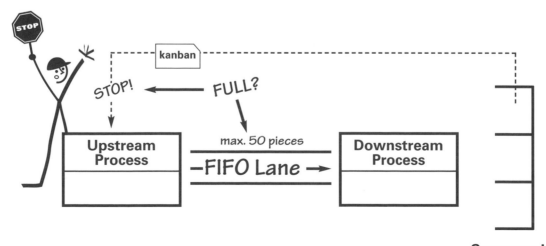

Guideline #4: Try to send the customer schedule to only one production process.

By using supermarket pull systems, you will typically need to schedule only one point in your door-to-door value stream. This point is called the **pacemaker process**, because how you control production at this process sets the pace for all the upstream processes. For example, fluctuations in production volume at the pacemaker process affect capacity requirements in upstream processes. Your selection of this scheduling point also determines what elements of your value stream become part of the lead time from customer order to finished goods.

Note that material transfers from the pacemaker process downstream to finished goods need to occur as a flow (no supermarkets or pulls downstream of the pacemaker process). Because of this, the pacemaker process is frequently the most downstream continuous-flow process in the door-to-door value stream. On the future-state map the pacemaker is the production process that is controlled by the outside customer's orders.

selecting the "Pacemaker Process"

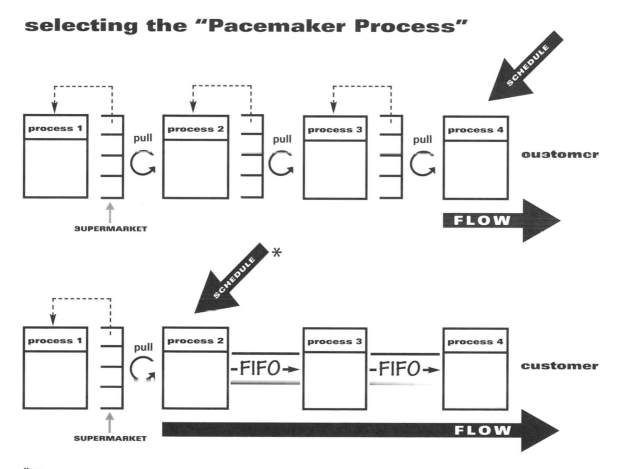

*Note:

With custom products and job shops, the scheduling point often needs to be further upstream like this.

Guideline #5: Distribute the production of different products evenly over time at the pacemaker process. (Level the production mix)

Most assembly departments probably find it easier to schedule long runs of one product type and avoid changeovers, but this creates serious problems for the rest of the value stream.

Grouping the same products and producing them all at once makes it difficult to serve customers who want something different from the batch being produced now. This requires you to have more finished goods inventory—in the hope that you will have on hand what a customer wants—or more lead time to fulfill an order.

Batching in assembly also means that fabricated components will be consumed in batches, which swells the in-process inventories needed in upstream supermarkets throughout the entire value stream. And, because variation in a final assembly schedule is amplified as you move upstream, those in-process inventories will tend to grow larger the further upstream you go.

Leveling the product mix means distributing the production of different products evenly over a time period. For example, instead of assembling all the "Type A" products in the morning and all the "Type B" in the afternoon, leveling means alternating repeatedly between smaller batches of "A" and "B".

The more you level the product mix at the pacemaker process, the more able you will be to respond to different customer requirements with a short lead time while holding little finished goods inventory. This also allows your upstream supermarkets to be smaller. But be warned that leveling the mix requires taking some pains in assembly, such as more changeovers and trying to keep all component variations at the line at all times (to eliminate changeover time). Your reward is the elimination of large amounts of waste in the value stream.

The icon for leveling is this symbol, which is inserted into an information flow arrow.

 Load Leveling

Guideline #6: Create an "initial pull" by releasing and withdrawing small, consistent increments of work at the pacemaker process. (Level the production volume)

Too many companies release large batches of work to their shop floor processes, which causes several problems:

- There is no sense of takt time (no "takt image") and no "pull" to which the value stream can respond.
- The volume of work performed typically occurs unevenly over time, with peaks and valleys that cause extra burden on machines, people, and supermarkets.
- The situation becomes difficult to monitor: "Are we behind or ahead?"
- With a large amount of work released to the shop floor, each process in the value stream can shuffle orders. This increases lead time and the need to expedite.
- Responding to changes in customer requirements becomes very complicated, which can often be seen in very complex information flows in current-state drawings.

Establishing a consistent, or level production pace creates a predictable production flow, which by its nature advises you of problems and enables you to take quick corrective action. A good place to start is to regularly release only a small, consistent amount of production instruction (usually between 5-60 minutes worth) at the pacemaker process, and simultaneously take away an equal amount of finished goods. We call this practice a "paced withdrawal".

We call the consistent increment of work the **pitch**, and often calculate the pitch increment based on packout container quantity (the number of parts one finished-goods container holds), or a multiple or fraction of that quantity. For example: If your **takt time** = 30 seconds, and your **pack size** = 20 pieces, then your **pitch** = 10 minutes (30 sec x 20 pcs = 10 minutes). In other words every 10 minutes:

    a) give the pacemaker process instruction to produce one pack quantity;
    b) take away one finished pitch quantity.

So in this case pitch means multiplying your takt time upward to a finished-goods transfer quantity at the pacemaker process. This then becomes the basic unit of your production schedule for a product family.

What is your management time frame?

- What increment of work are you releasing?
- How often do you know your performance to customer demand?

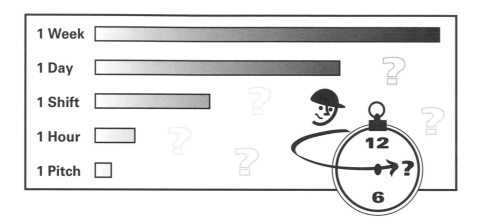

One way to think about pitch is as your "management time frame". How often do you know your performance to customer demand? If you release a week of work to the floor at one time, then the answer is probably "once a week". It is impossible to produce to takt time in this situation. There is no "takt image"! However, if you are scheduling and checking production every pitch, then you can rapidly respond to problems and maintain takt time. Just as we don't want to transfer material in large batches, we don't want to transfer production instruction (information) in big batches either.

load-leveling box
kanban are responded to from left to right at pitch increment

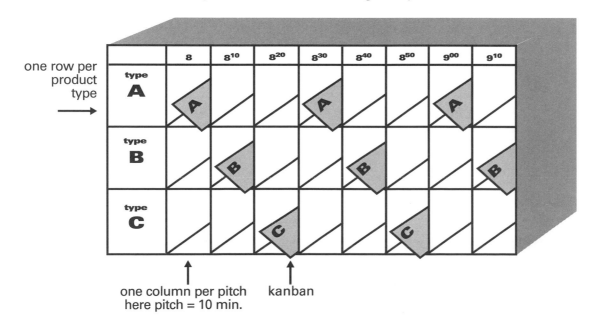

There are many ways to practice paced withdrawal of small, consistent quantities of work. A tool used at some companies to help level both the mix and volume of production is a load-leveling (or heijunka) box. A load-leveling box has a column of kanban slots for each pitch interval, and a row of kanban slots for each product type. In this system kanban indicate not only the quantity to be produced, but also how long it takes to produce that quantity (based on takt time). Kanban are placed (loaded) into the leveling box in the desired mix sequence by product type (see leveling box illustration). The material handler then withdraws those kanban and brings them to the pacemaker process—one at a time, at the pitch increment.

The icon for leveling the production pace is the same symbol as for leveling the mix (see Guideline #5 above), because a pre-requisite for lean manufacturing is that both the mix and volume of production be leveled.

an example of "Paced Withdrawal"

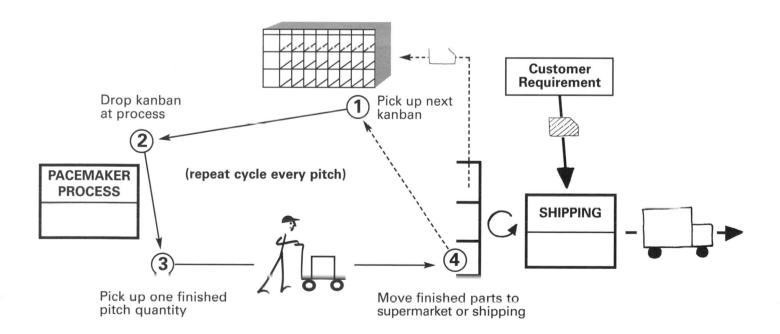

Guideline 7: Develop the ability to make "every part every day" (then every shift, then every hour or pallet or pitch) in fabrication processes upstream of the pacemaker process.

By shortening changeover times and running smaller batches in your upstream fabrication processes, those processes will be able to respond to changing downstream needs more quickly. In turn they will require even less inventory to be held in their supermarkets. This applies to both discrete-parts manufacturing and process industries.

In general, we note either the batch sizes or "EPEx" in the data boxes. EPEx stands for "every part every…" after which you write a time such as week, day, shift, hour, pitch, or takt. This describes how frequently a process changes over to produce all part variations. An initial goal at many plants is to make at least "every part every <u>day</u>" for high-running part numbers.

Note:

One method for determining initial batch sizes at fabrication processes is to base them on how much time you have left in the day to make changeovers.

For example, if you have 16 hours available per day and it takes 14.5 hours to run the daily requirement, then there are 1.5 hours available for changeovers. (A typical target is approximately 10% of available time to be used for changeovers.) In this case if the current changeover time is 15 minutes, then you can make 6 changeovers per day. To run smaller batches more frequently you will need to reduce the changeover time and/or improve uptime.

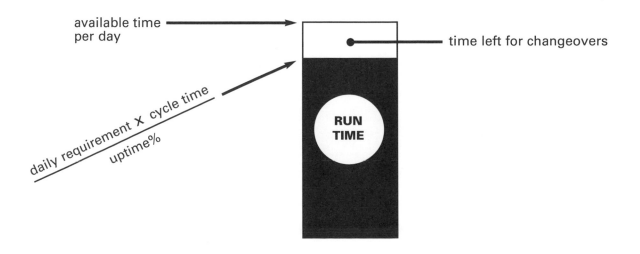

PART IV: THE FUTURE-STATE MAP

- Drawing the Future-State Map
- Your Turn

PART IV: THE FUTURE-STATE MAP

- Drawing the Future-State Map
- Your Turn

FUTURE-STATE MAP

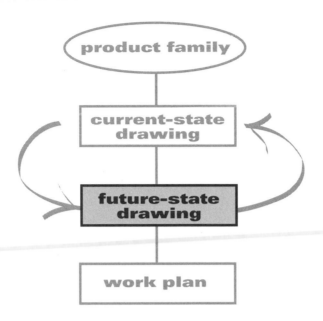

The Future-State Map

The purpose of value-stream mapping is to highlight sources of waste and eliminate them by implementation of a future-state value stream that can become a reality within a short period of time. The goal is to build a chain of production where the individual processes are linked to their customer(s) either by continuous flow or pull, and each process gets as close as possible to producing only what its customer(s) need when they need it.

Assuming you are working at an existing facility with an existing product and process, some of the waste in a value stream will be the result of the product's design, the processing machinery already bought, and the remote location of some activities. These features of the current state probably can't be changed immediately. Unless you are involved in a new product introduction, the first iteration of your future-state map should take product designs, process technologies, and plant locations as given and seek to remove as quickly as possible all sources of waste not caused by these features. (With the exception of minor purchases think, *"What can we do with what we have?"*) Subsequent iterations can address your product design, technology, and location issues.

We have found that the most useful aid for helping people draw future-state maps is the following list of questions. As you develop your future-state concepts, answer the questions in roughly the following order. Based on your answers to these questions, mark your future-state ideas directly on your current-state map in red pencil. Once you have worked out your future-state thoughts in this way, you can draw a future-state map.

KEY QUESTIONS FOR THE FUTURE STATE

1) <u>What is the takt time</u>, based on the available working time of your downstream processes that are closest to the customer?

2) <u>Will you build to a finished goods supermarket from which the customer pulls, or directly to shipping?</u> (The answer to this question depends on several factors such as customer buying patterns, the reliability of your processes, and the characteristics of your product. Building directly to shipping will require either a reliable, short-lead-time, order-to-delivery stream, or more safety stock. Fortunately, your order-to-delivery lead time involves only those processes from the pacemaker process downstream to delivery.)

3) <u>Where can you use continuous flow processing?</u>

4) <u>Where will you need to use supermarket pull systems</u> in order to control production of upstream processes?

5) <u>At what single point in the production chain (the "pacemaker process") will you schedule production?</u> (Remember that all material transfers downstream of the pacemaker process need to occur as a flow.)

6) <u>How will you level the production mix</u> at the pacemaker process?

7) <u>What increment of work will you consistently release</u> and take away at the pacemaker process?

8) <u>What process improvements will be necessary</u> for the value stream to flow as your future-state design specifies? (This is the place to note any equipment and procedural improvements that will be necessary, such as reducing changeover time or improving machine uptime. We use the kaizen lightning burst icon to indicate these points in the process.)

Changeover

Drawing the Future-State Map

When we look again at the current-state map for Acme's steering column bracket, what problems do we note? Perhaps the most striking are the large amounts of inventory, the unconnected processes (each producing to its own schedule) pushing their output forward, and the long lead time in comparison to the short processing time. What can be done about this? We'll let the key questions be our guide.

Question #1: What is Acme's takt time for the chosen product family?

The takt time calculation starts with the available working time for one shift in Acme's assembly area, which is 28,800 seconds (8 hours). From this you subtract any non-working time, which is two 10 minute breaks per shift. The customer demand of 460 units per shift is then divided into the available working time to give a takt of 60 seconds.

Available Working Time: 28,800 - 1200 = 27,600 seconds per shift

$$\frac{\text{Available Working Time}}{\text{Customer Demand}} \qquad 27,600 \text{ sec.} \div 460 \text{ units per shift}$$

Acme Steering Bracket Assembly Takt Time = 60 seconds

What this takt time number means is that in order to meet customer demand within its available work time, Acme needs to produce a steering bracket every 60 seconds in its assembly process. This number includes no time for equipment downtime, changeovers between left-drive and right-drive brackets, or for producing scrap. Acme may decide to cycle assembly faster than takt, if it cannot immediately eliminate downtime problems for example, but the takt time is a reference number defined by the customer and cannot be changed by Acme Stamping.

Note:

Try to cycle your pacemaker process as close as possible to takt time. A significant gap between takt time and cycle time indicates the existence of production problems that cause unplanned downtime. When you compensate for production problems by cycling much faster than takt, the incentive to eliminate those problems evaporates. If you cycle faster than takt there should be a plan for closing the gap.

Question #2: Should Acme build steering brackets to a finished goods supermarket or directly to shipping?

At Acme, steering brackets are small (easy to store) parts that have only two varieties. The customer's demand rises and falls somewhat unpredictably, and Acme is uncertain about the reliability of future-state changes to be made. So Acme has opted to begin with a finished goods supermarket and to move closer to "produce to shipping" in the future.

Acme can use the customer's thirty day forecast to determine the amount of production capacity needed in the period immediately ahead. (Lean plants periodically adjust the number of operators in assembly — and re-distribute the work elements — to match output to changes in demand.) Acme will determine actual production by means of kanban coming back upstream to the weld/assembly cell from the finished goods supermarket.

Since the customer buys in multiples of 20-bracket trays, this is the simple choice for "kanban size." That is, each tray of twenty left-drive or right-drive brackets in the finished-goods supermarket has on it one production kanban. As the shipping department withdraws trays from the supermarket to stage them for delivery, the kanban from those trays are sent back to assembly. Each of those kanban essentially says, "The customer has just consumed twenty left-drive (or right-drive) brackets, please make another 20."

Note:

For custom products you may not be able to create a supermarket of finished goods. (See diagram at bottom of page 49.)

Example: Building to a Supermarket
The supermarket schedules assembly (Acme's choice)

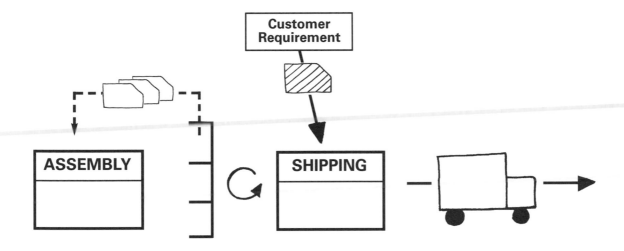

Example: Building Directly to Shipping
Production Control schedules assembly

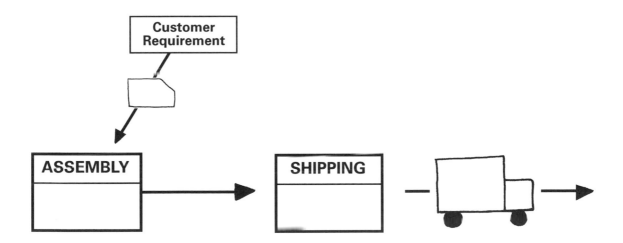

Question #3: Where can Acme introduce continuous flow?

The "operator-balance chart" below summarizes the current total cycle times for each process. The stamping operation cycles very quickly (1 second per part) and changes over to serve several product lines. So incorporating it into a continuous flow, which would mean slowing its cycle to near takt time and dedicating it to the steering bracket product family, is not practical. That would result in a vastly underutilized press and the need to buy another expensive stamping press for Acme's other product lines! It makes more sense to run Acme's stamping press as a batch operation and control its production with a supermarket-based pull system.

Examining the two assembly workstations, we notice that their cycle times are not too far apart and near the takt time as well. These workstations are also already dedicated to the steering bracket product family, so continuous flow in assembly certainly is a possibility. The same is true for the two welding workstations, where work could also pass directly from one welding step to the next in a continuous flow.

What prevents Acme from using continuous flow all the way from welding through assembly, a condition with no inventory (or a maximum of one piece at automated processes) between steps? In fact nothing. The lean approach is to place these four processes immediately adjacent to each other (typically in a cellular arrangement), have the operators carry or pass parts from one process step to the next, and distribute the work elements so that each operator's work content is just below takt time.

Acme stamping current cycle times

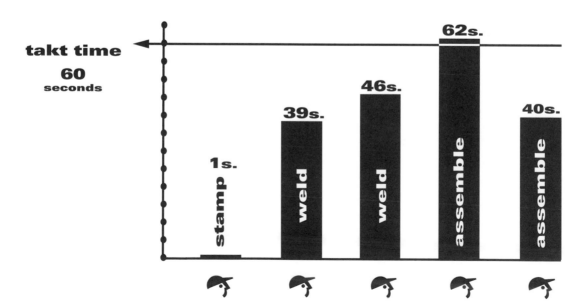

Dividing the total welding and assembly work content by the takt time (187 seconds divided by 60) reveals that 3.12 operators would be needed to run welding and assembly in a continuous flow at takt. Four operators would be quite underutilized, but a redistribution of work elements will not be sufficient to eliminate the need for a fourth operator.

Our next option is to eliminate waste through process kaizen to bring the work content under the takt time ceiling. A kaizen target might be to reduce each operator's work content to 55 seconds or less (or ≤165 seconds total work content.) If that fails, use of some overtime may be necessary. With either approach, the fourth operator and the material handler who currently moves parts between the isolated processes can be reassigned to other activities that actually create value.

To allow production to takt time and mix leveling, a pacemaker process should ideally incur little or no changeover time and change over very frequently. So the left-drive to right-drive welding-fixture changeover times will need to be reduced from the current ten minutes to a few seconds. Focused attention on improving the reliability of the second spot welder (perhaps through an improved maintenance approach) will also be needed.

Acme stamping
weld/assembly cell cycle times after process kaizen

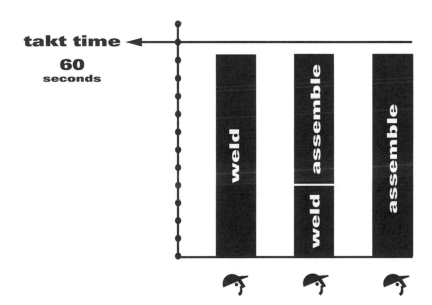

Notice that on this future-state map the four welding and assembly process boxes have been combined into one process box to indicate the continuous flow. A small schematic sketch of a cell inside the process box also indicates the cellular manufacturing idea.

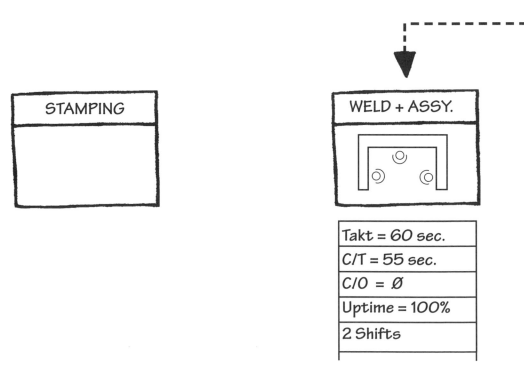

First View of the Future-State Map Showing Takt Time, Weld/Assembly Cell, and the Finished-Goods Supermarket

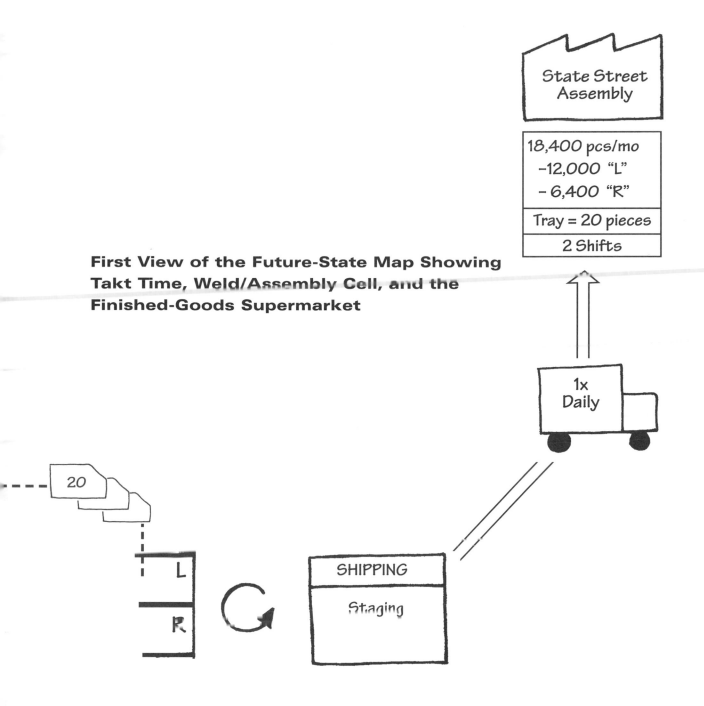

State Street
Assembly

| 18,400 pcs/mo |
| –12,000 "L" |
| – 6,400 "R" |
| Tray = 20 pieces |
| 2 Shifts |

1x
Daily

20

L

R

SHIPPING

Staging

Question #4. Where will Acme need to use supermarket pull systems?

Acme has decided to produce steering brackets to a finished-goods supermarket
(see Question #2). Two additional supermarkets — one for stamped parts and one for coils —
are necessary to complete Acme's in-plant value stream for steering brackets.

Stamped Parts

Ideally we might introduce a tiny stamping machine dedicated to steering brackets — what
we call a "right sized tool" — and incorporate this mini-press into the welding and assembly
continuous flow. Unfortunately, this is not possible in the immediate future because machinery
of this type does not yet exist. So we need to set up a supermarket and use withdrawals from
that supermarket (pull) to control stamping's production of left-drive and right-drive parts.

Pull system design begins with customer requirements, and stamping's customer here is
the weld/assembly cell. The cell currently requires approximately 600 LH and 320 RH
stamped parts per day. Containers for the stamped parts should be sized to allow close-to-
the-fingertips placement in the cell (for example plastic bins that fit into gravity-feed racks
near the operators), not primarily for the convenience of the stamping or material handling
departments! Small containers allow Acme to keep both LH and RH stamped parts in the
cell at all times. This further reduces LH-to-RH changeover time at the pacemaker
process, where very frequent changeovers (leveling the mix) is a key lean objective.

Each container in the cell — for example a bin that holds 60 stamped parts, or about one
hour of current steering bracket assembly — will have a withdrawal kanban with it. When a
cell operator begins taking parts out of another bin, its withdrawal kanban is given to the
material handler so that he/she knows to go to the stamping supermarket and "withdraw"
another bin of those parts.

Withdrawal kanban trigger the movement of parts. *Production kanban* trigger the production
of parts. Acme can attach a production kanban to each bin of 60 stamped parts in the
supermarket. Every time the material handler removes a bin from the supermarket a
kanban will be sent back to the stamping press. This instructs stamping to produce 60
parts, place them in a bin, and move it to a specified location (the "market address") in
the stamping supermarket.

Now stamping no longer receives a schedule from production control. With mapping icons the flow looks like this:

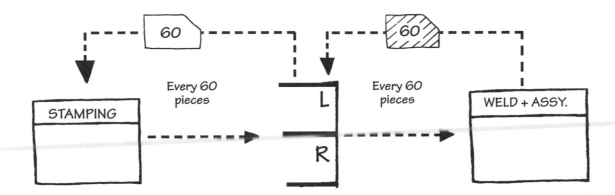

However, you may have already noticed a problem with this pull system. With a cycle time of one second per piece and a changeover time of one hour, stamping would take one hour to set up to run only 60 seconds (60 pieces) of production. Until changeover time on the stamping press is greatly reduced, replenishing what is withdrawn from the stamping supermarket on a bin-for-bin basis is clearly not practical.

Due to changeover time, stamping needs to produce batches larger than 60 pieces between changeovers. With the initial goal of "every part every day", stamping's target batch size for steering brackets would be approximately 600 LH and 320 RH pieces (which will still require changeover-time reduction). Stamping will keep 1.5 days of parts in its supermarket, one half day extra to allow for replenishment delay and some stamping problems.

So Acme will use a *signal* kanban to schedule stamping. In this case the kanban (often a metal triangle) for left- and right-drive parts is brought from the supermarket to the stamping press whenever the number of bins remaining in the supermarket drops to a trigger ("minimum") point. When a triangle kanban arrives at the stamping press' scheduling board, it initiates a changeover and production of a predetermined batch size of a specific part. Stamping still does not receive a schedule from production control.

Drawn with icons, the flow now looks like this:

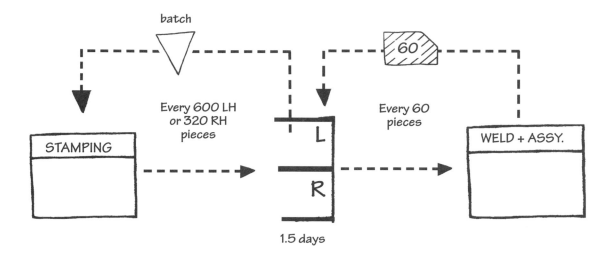

The stamped-parts supermarket, withdrawal and signal kanban, and kanban flows (dotted lines) are drawn on the future state map.

Coils

To build a plant-level lean value stream the future state map must also show a third supermarket at the receiving dock, which holds coils of steel. Even though Acme's steel supplier is not ready to receive kanban and produce according to them, Acme can still attach an internal withdrawal kanban to every coil and send those kanban to its own production control department whenever another coil is used. Production control can then order coils based on actual usage, instead of based on MRP's best guess of what future usage will be. (MRP may still be used to provide a capacity-planning forecast for the coil supplier, but day-to-day orders should be based on pull.)

Once production control has made the day's order for coils, the corresponding kanban can be placed in kanban slots at the receiving dock. These indicate the day that coils should arrive. If there are kanban still left in yesterday's receiving slot, then something is wrong at the supplier.

Currently the steel supplier is shipping coils weekly. By lining up other customers along a "milk run" delivery, it may be possible to get the necessary amount of steel on a daily basis, even if the steel supplier does nothing to reduce its minimum batch size for slitting coils. Simply moving to daily delivery eliminates 80% of the inventory at Acme, while providing smooth, steady demand for the steel supplier.

Our Progress So Far

We have now proposed a cell of the type many firms have implemented in the past few years, the introduction of pull to control stamping production and coil delivery, "every part every day" in stamping, and instituting milk runs for delivery from the raw material supplier to Acme. By constructing a "before-and-after" table (see below) for the current state and the future state so far, we can see that a large amount of waste can be removed through these actions.

These are big steps forward. However, if the rest of the information flow at Acme is not fundamentally changed, it will be very difficult to operate a lean value stream. So we need to go back to the customer and rethink the flow of information about customer desires as it is sent back to Acme and used there.

Acme Stamping Lead Time Improvement

	Coils	Stamped Parts	Weld/Assy WIP	Finished Goods	Production Lead Time	Total Inventory Turns
Before	5 Days	7.6 Days	6.5 Days	4.5 Days	23.6 Days	10
So Far	2 Days	1.5 Days	Ø	4.5 Days	8 Days	30

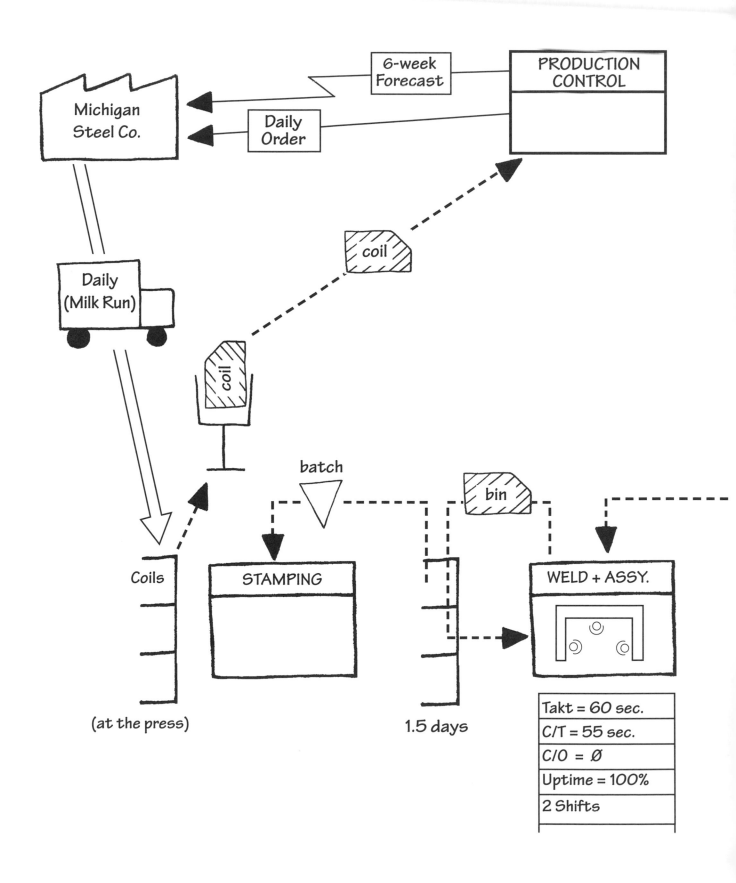

Second View of the Future-State Map Showing Stamping and Raw Material Supermarkets

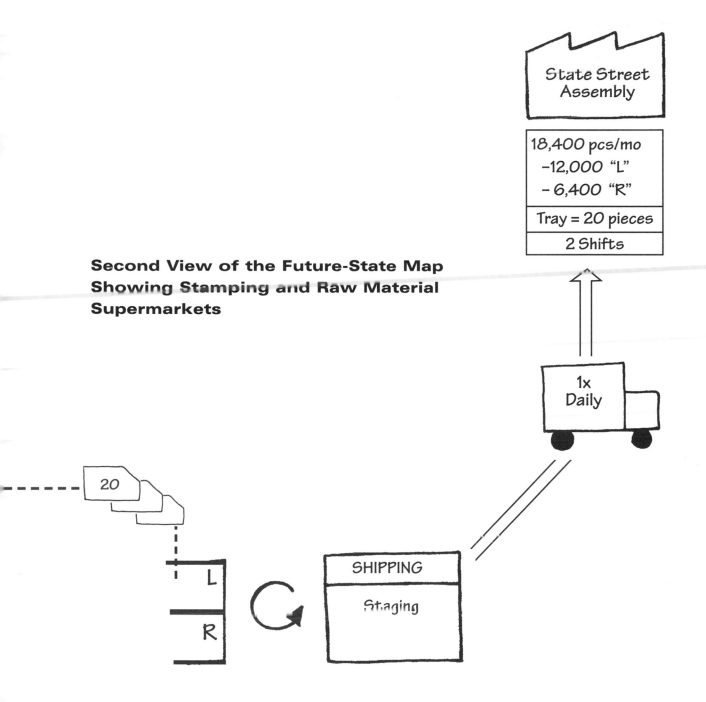

State Street Assembly

| 18,400 pcs/mo |
| −12,000 "L" |
| − 6,400 "R" |
| Tray = 20 pieces |
| 2 Shifts |

1x Daily

20

L

R

SHIPPING

Staging

How can we flow information so that one process will make only what the next process needs when it needs it?

Years ago, Toyota discovered a very different method of managing the schedule: stop trying to guess what the customer will want. Instead, shorten lead times within production and install supermarkets with small inventories of each product between processes that cannot be coupled to one another. These will permit upstream processes to simply replace in the supermarket what downstream processes have just withdrawn. Then, instead of sending customer information to a centralized MRP system, which then sends instructions to each production activity, level the customer orders and send them only to one place — either directly to the pacemaker process, where the requested products will be produced in time for shipment, or to a finished goods supermarket, where the requested products will be withdrawn and staged for shipment.

Currently, the customer is sending by fax a ninety-day forecast, revised once a month and frozen at thirty days. In addition, it is sending a daily release during the night by EDI (Electronic Data Interchange — in plain language, by phone line) to Acme's scheduling computer for the next day's shipping requirement. Finally, there are occasional revisions in shipping requirements on an emergency basis. These are sent by phone from the customer's material handling department to Acme's shipping department during the day as the assembly plant discovers that needed parts are not on hand for whatever reason.

What happens to the information sent from the customer once it reaches Acme? In the current case, the weekly schedule is fed over the weekend into the computerized MRP which then sends instructions by Monday morning to each department—stamping, welding I & II, and assembly I & II — about what to make the coming week. Then, as additional information is received each night and as each department reports back periodically to the MRP on what it actually did that day (because production does not go as scheduled), the daily production schedules are continually adjusted to bring what Acme is making into synch with what the customer wants.

If this sounds complicated it is because trying to run operations off of MRP systems doesn't work well. There is still a frequent need for humans to override the system to avoid shortages at various stages of production. The occasional call from the customer for emergency changes in orders requires human intervention as well and upsets the entire production schedule, requiring recalculation and retransmission to the processing areas.

Question #5: What single point in the production chain (the pacemaker process) should Acme schedule?

Since all process steps downstream of the pacemaker process need to occur in a flow, in the Acme example the scheduling point is clearly the welding/assembly cell. We cannot schedule any further upstream (at the stamping process) because we are planning to introduce a pull system between stamping and weld/assembly. This single scheduling point will regulate Acme's entire steering-bracket value stream.

Question #6: How should Acme level the production mix at the pacemaker process?

When the daily delivery is made to the assembly plant, 30 trays of left-drive brackets (600 pieces) and 16 trays of right-drive brackets (320 pieces) are typically staged and loaded onto the truck at one time. If we are not careful, the 46 production kanban removed from these trays before loading will be sent back to the weld/assembly cell in a batch, as shown on the future-state map so far. If this happens the weld/assembly cell will probably batch-produce these parts. That is, the cell will produce all 30 trays of left-drive brackets, and then change over to make the 16 trays of right-drive brackets, which would look like this:

1st Shift   **2nd Shift**

LLLLLLLLLLLLLLLLLLLLLLLLLLLLLLRRRRRRRRRRRRRRRR

From the cell's perspective this seems to make sense because it minimizes the number of required weld-fixture changes. However, from a value-stream perspective batching is the wrong way to go. Batch-producing brackets in assembly will increase the impact of problems, lengthen the lead time, and mean that the stamped-parts supermarket has to be ready to meet sudden demand surges. "Being ready" means keeping more stamped parts inventory in the supermarket, which again increases lead time, obscures stamping's quality problems and, in general, causes all those wastes associated with overproduction.

Instead, if the weld/assembly cell levels the mix of brackets it produces evenly over the shift, then the stamping press (with a shortened setup time) will have plenty of time to react to the cell's pulls for left-drive and right-drive parts. It will have time to replenish what was taken away without the need for so much inventory in the stamping supermarket.

With leveling, which requires much more frequent changeovers, the cell's production mix of trays of brackets would look like this:

1st Shift   **2nd Shift**

RLLRLLRLLRLLRLLRLLRLLRLLRLLRLLRLLRLLRLLRLLRLLR

Note:

Enabling such frequent changeovers in the cell will probably require keeping all fixtures and component varieties ready, near the operator's fingertips. However, when all components are kept on the line you may need some failsafe devices to prevent the wrong ones from being assembled.

Here the benefit of a value-stream perspective should become evident to you. By taking a few pains to level the production mix at the pacemaker process, which may seem unnatural at that location, the entire value stream will show improved lead time, quality, and cost. As you can imagine, these benefits are amplified greatly in value streams that are longer and more complex than our Acme example.

How can we ensure that kanban coming back to the weld/assembly cell, which are the production instructions, come back in a sequence that levels the mix of products over the shift? At Acme there are two places where the batch of kanban can be intercepted and this leveling can take place. (We'll assume that Acme has decided to use a load-leveling box to help maintain a level production mix, paced withdrawal, and genuine pull.)

Option A. Production control can place withdrawal ("move") kanban corresponding to the customer order in a load-leveling box near the shipping dock in a mixed, left- drive/right-drive sequence. A material handler then pulls these kanban out of the leveling box one-by-one at the pitch increment (20 minutes in this case), and moves trays of brackets from the finished goods supermarket to the staging area one-by-one according to the withdrawal kanban.

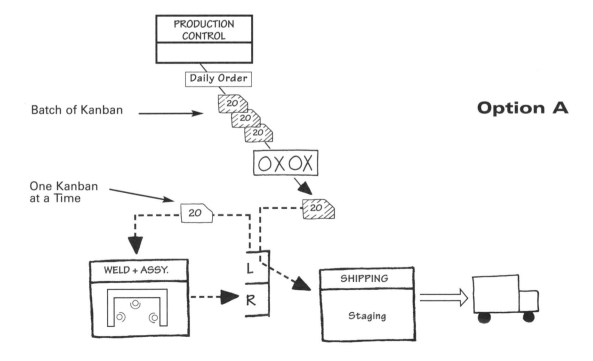

As each tray is pulled from the supermarket, the production kanban on those trays are brought back to the cell in time increments and a left-drive/right-drive pattern that mirrors exactly the mix and pitch increment that production control had set up. (This leveling option is the one shown in Acme's completed future-state map.)

Option B. Production control can send today's customer order to the material handler, who pulls all the corresponding trays out of the finished goods market at once and stages them for shipment. Pulling the trays produces a batch of production kanban, which are placed in a load leveling box near the cell, in a mixed, left-drive/right-drive sequence. The weld/ assembly material handler then pulls production kanban out of the leveling device one at a time at the pitch increment and as a result assembly produces in a left-drive/right-drive mixed pattern.

The drawback of Option B compared to Option A is that in B an entire batch of finished goods is moved to shipping at once. Lean manufacturing strives to avoid or minimize batching as much as possible, always getting closer and closer to continuous flow. Also, if Acme is someday able to shrink its finished-goods supermarket to less than one day of inventory, withdrawing a one-day quantity all at once will not be possible. However, Option A does require someone to repeatedly move one tray at a time (at the pitch increment) not only from the weld/assembly cell to the finished goods supermarket, but also from finished goods to the shipping dock.

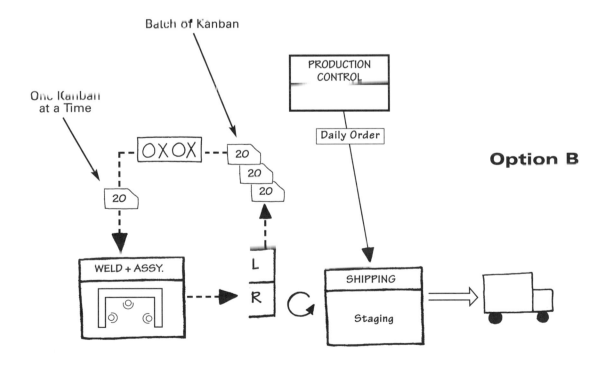

Question #7: What consistent increment of work should Acme release and take away at the pacemaker process?

How will Acme provide takt image to the weld/assembly cell, and how frequently will it check production there? Returning all 46 kanban (two shifts worth) to the cell at once would provide no takt image to the cell. Batching the volume of work instruction like this must be avoided. A natural increment of welding/assembly work in Acme's case is the 60 second takt time x 20 pieces per tray = 20 minutes. This is the steering-bracket **pitch**, which corresponds to one kanban for one tray of 20 steering brackets.

Does this mean that every 20 minutes someone walks over to the weld/assembly cell and asks, "How are things going?" Not exactly. What this pitch means is that Acme will practice paced release of work instruction, one kanban at a time, and paced withdrawal of finished goods at its weld/assembly cell.

Each column in Acme's steering-bracket load-leveling box represents a 20-minute pitch increment. The two rows are designated for left-drive and right-drive kanban. Every 20 minutes, a material handler brings the next kanban (the next increment of work) to the weld/assembly cell and moves the just-finished tray of brackets to the finished goods area. If a tray is not finished at the 20-minute pitch increment, then Acme knows there is a production problem (for example a problem with the spot welding equipment) that needs attention.

Acme load-leveling box for steering brackets
weld/assembly cell gets kanban from left to right at pitch increment

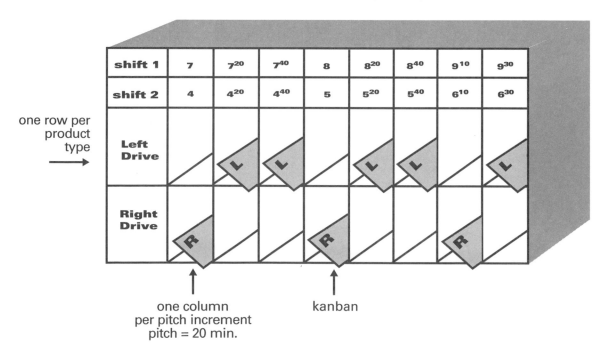

Question #8: What process improvements will be necessary for Acme's value stream to flow as the future-state design describes?

Achieving the material and information flows we envision for Acme Stamping requires the following process improvements:

- Reduction in changeover time and batch sizes at the stamping press, to allow faster response to downstream usage. The goals are "every part every day" and then "every part every shift".

- Elimination of the long time (10 minutes) required to change between left-drive and right-drive fixtures in welding, to make possible continuous flow and mixed production from welding through assembly.

- Improvement in on-demand uptime of the second spot-weld machine, as it will now be tied to other processes in a continuous flow.

- Elimination of waste in the weld/assembly cell, to reduce total work content down to 165 seconds or less. (Which allows use of 3 operators at the current demand level.)

We mark these items on our future-state map with the kaizen lightening burst icon.

We should also figure out how to use the existing stamping technology — designed to produce stampings in much higher volume than the customer for this product desires — in a less wasteful way. The secret here is to have the stamping press, which also stamps parts for other product families in the plant, make smaller batches of the two parts our value stream needs and make them more frequently. This will require additional reduction of the changeover time.

In fact, the methods for reducing set up times on a stamping press are well known and a reduction in time to less than ten minutes can be achieved quickly. With that, we can imagine the press making only about 300 left-drive stampings and 160 right-drive stampings (the per-shift production need); then producing parts for other value streams; then making more lefts and rights on the next shift.

EPE will now equal every part every <u>shift</u>! This way the amount of inventory stored between the stamping process and the weld/assembly cell would be reduced by about 85 percent.

We can now draw Acme's complete future-state value-stream map, with information flows, material flows, and kaizen needs specified.

 **GO LOOK!**

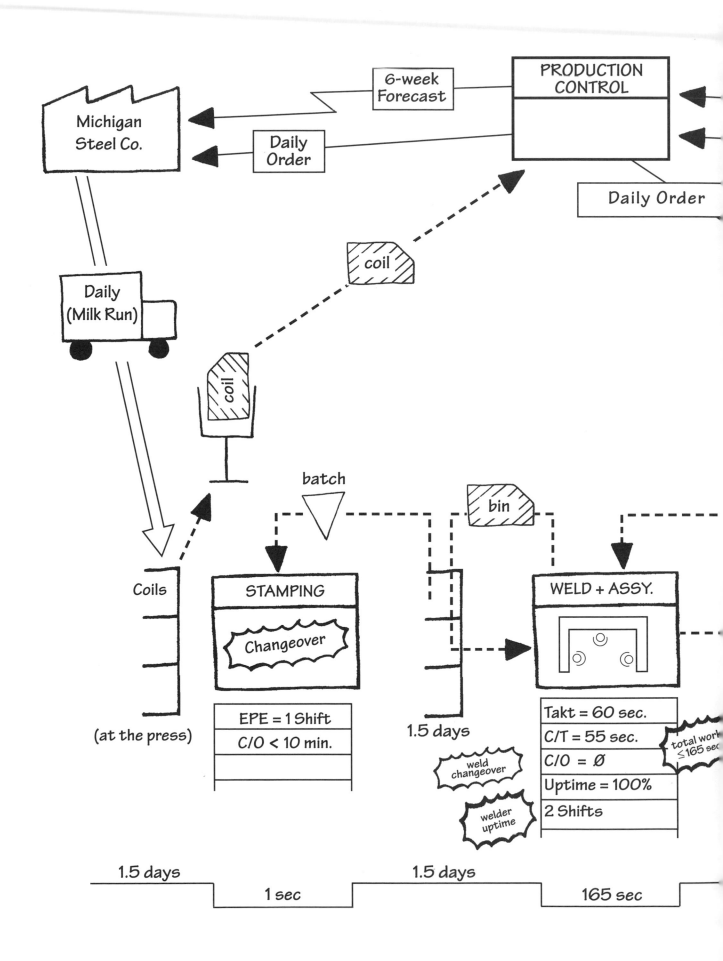

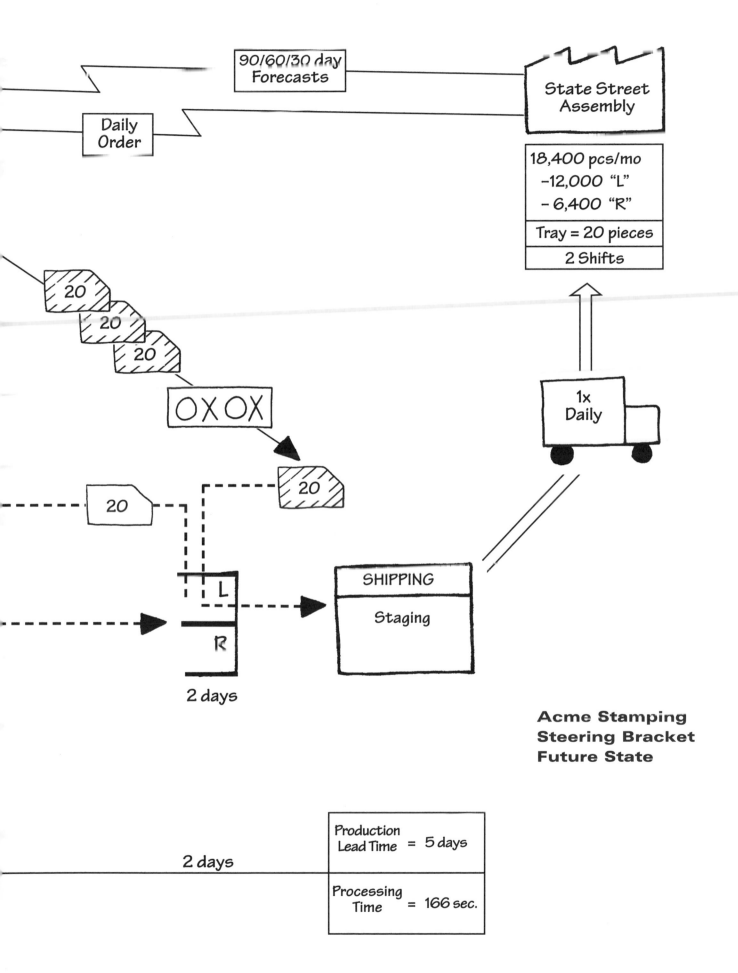

90/60/30 day Forecasts

Daily Order

State Street Assembly

18,400 pcs/mo
–12,000 "L"
– 6,400 "R"

Tray = 20 pieces

2 Shifts

20

20

20

OXOX

20

20

L

R

2 days

1x Daily

SHIPPING

Staging

Acme Stamping
Steering Bracket
Future State

2 days

Production Lead Time = 5 days

Processing Time = 166 sec.

The beauty of asking question #8 last is that your process-improvement efforts become subordinate to the overall value-stream design, as opposed to vague, stand-alone improvement activities. Teams can now be dispatched to work on these process improvements with a clear understanding of why they are making these improvements.

However, be sure to kick off these improvement projects by creating a "pull" for the improvements. That is, instead of "pushing" a team to reduce setup time on the stamping press, begin instead by stating that in 30 days the batch sizes on the stamping press will be reduced to 300 & 160 pieces. This creates a sense of urgency about making the process improvement. Likewise, don't simply send a team to eliminate the weld-fixture changeover time and wait for them to be finished. Begin by stating that in 14 days the welding and assembly steps will be placed into a continuous flow orientation.

Summing Up

When we compare the summary statistics for Acme's current state and its future state, the results are quite striking. In particular, due to leveling production in its weld/assembly cell and developing the ability to stamp every part every shift, Acme can further reduce the amount of coils and stamped parts held in supermarkets. Of course, this puts great pressure on maintaining equipment reliability and predictability of production to takt.

With the shortened production lead time through its shop floor, the pacemaker process operating consistently to takt time, and fast response to problems, Acme can comfortably reduce the amount of finished goods it holds to two days. (If Acme's customer were to level its schedule, this finished goods inventory could be reduced even further.)

Compared with the interim improvements shown in the table, leveling production at Acme has further reduced production lead time by another 3 days and nearly doubled inventory turns.

Acme Stamping Lead-Time Improvement

	Coils	Stamped Parts	Weld/Assy WIP	Finished Goods	Production Lead Time	Total Inventory Turns
Before	5 Days	7.6 Days	6.5 Days	4.5 Days	23.6 Days	10
Continuous Flow & Pull	2 Days	1.5 Days	Ø	4.5 Days	8 Days	30
With Leveling	1.5 Days	1.5 Days	Ø	2 Days	5 Days	48

Your Turn

Before you head off to create the future state for your own value streams — which we hope and trust you will do very shortly — you may need some practice. We invite you to take another clean sheet of paper and draw a future-state value-stream map for the "TWI Industries" example on page 35 you used to practice creating a current-state value stream. You can compare your future-state map with our map by turning to Appendix C.

Remember that what is "right" in terms of a value-stream map is one that permits you to quickly remove root causes of waste. Therefore, please take our map and mapping techniques as a provocative suggestion and revise the basic ideas to suit your particular needs.

PART V: ACHIEVING THE FUTURE STATE

- Breaking Implementation Into Steps

- The Value-Stream Plan

- Value-Stream Improvement
  is Management's Job

PART V: ACHIEVING THE FUTURE STATE

- • Breaking Implementation Into Steps
- • The Value-Stream Plan
- • Value-Stream Improvement
  is Management's Job

Achieving the Future State

Value-stream mapping is only a tool. Unless you achieve the future state that you have drawn — and achieve parts of it within a short period of time — your value-stream maps are nearly worthless.

This final section of *Learning to See* discusses developing and using a yearly value-stream plan and ends with some management guidelines for developing lean value streams.

THE PLAN FOR ACHIEVING YOUR FUTURE-STATE VALUE STREAM CAN BE A COMPACT DOCUMENT THAT INCLUDES THE FOLLOWING ITEMS:

1) Future-state map

2) Any detailed process-level maps or layouts that are necessary

3) A yearly value-stream plan

Breaking Implementation into Steps

A value-stream map looks at the entire flow through your facility, as opposed to only individual processing areas, and in most cases it will not be possible to implement your entire future-state concept at once. There is too much to do! So it is the value-stream manager's responsibility to break implementation into steps.

Perhaps the most important point about your future-state implementation plan is not to think of it as implementing a series of techniques, but to envision it as a process of building a series of connected flows for a family of products. To help you do this, try to think about "value-stream loops."

Divide your future-state value-stream map into segments or loops, as described below and shown at right:

The Pacemaker Loop: The pacemaker loop encompasses the flow of material and information between your customer and your pacemaker process. This is the most downstream loop in your facility, and how you manage this loop impacts all the upstream processes in that value stream.

Additional Loops: Upstream of the pacemaker loop there are material-flow and information-flow loops between pulls. That is, each pull-system supermarket in your value stream usually corresponds with the end of another loop.

You can circle these loops on your future-state map, to help you see the flow segments that make up your value stream. These loops are an excellent way to break your future-state implementation effort into manageable pieces.

In the Acme Stamping future-state map there are three loops — pacemaker, stamping, and supplier — shown on page 89. With these three loops in mind, Acme's steering-bracket value-stream manager can break implementation into steps, by loop, which might look like page 88.

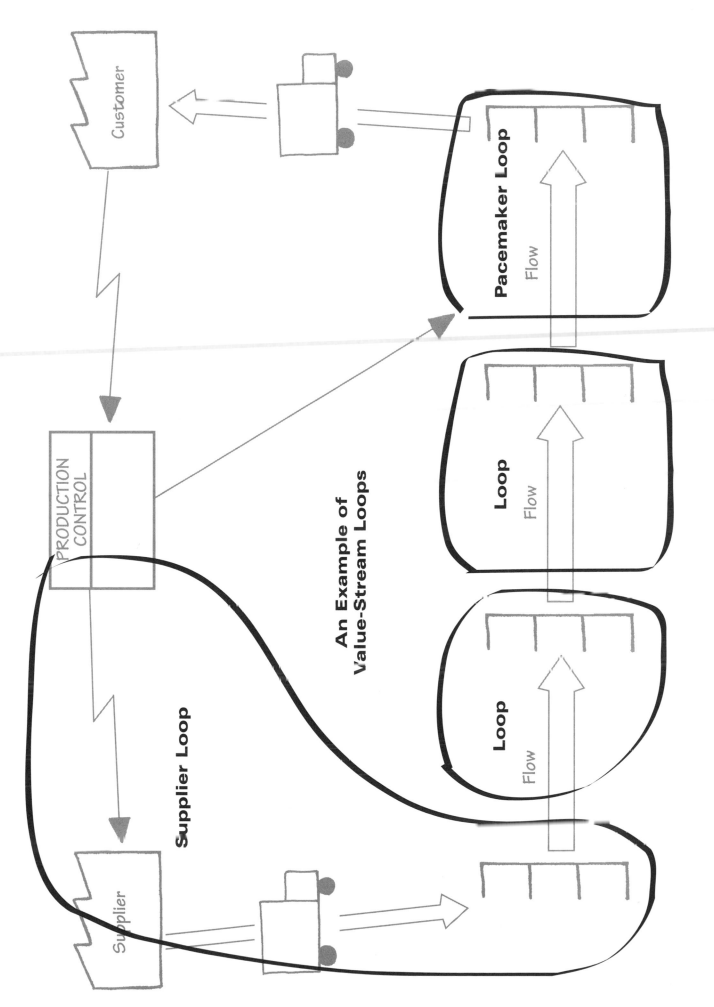

**An Example of
Value-Stream Loops**

Customer

PRODUCTION
CONTROL

Supplier

Supplier Loop

Pacemaker Loop

Flow

Loop

Flow

Loop

Flow

Acme Future-State Implementation Steps

Loop 1: Pacemaker loop

Objectives:

- develop continuous flow from weld through assembly (cell)
- kaizen work elements to reduce total cycle time to 165 seconds or less
- eliminate weld-fixture changeover time
- improve uptime on welder #2 to 100%
- develop pull system with finished-goods supermarket (eliminate schedules)
- develop material-handler routes between the supermarkets and the cell

Goals:

- only 2 days of finished goods inventory in supermarket
- no inventory between workstations
- operate the cell with 3 people (at current demand rate)

Loop 2: Stamping loop

Objectives:

- establish pull system with stamped-parts supermarket (eliminate stamping schedule)
- reduce stamping batch sizes to 300 (LH) and 160 (RH)
- reduce stamping changeover time to less than 10 minutes

Goals:

- only 1 day of stamped-bracket inventory in supermarket
- batch sizes of 300 & 160 pieces between changeovers

Loop 3: Coil-Supplier loop

Objectives:

- develop pull system with steel-coil supermarket
- introduce daily coil delivery

Goal:

- only 1.5 days of coil inventory in supermarket

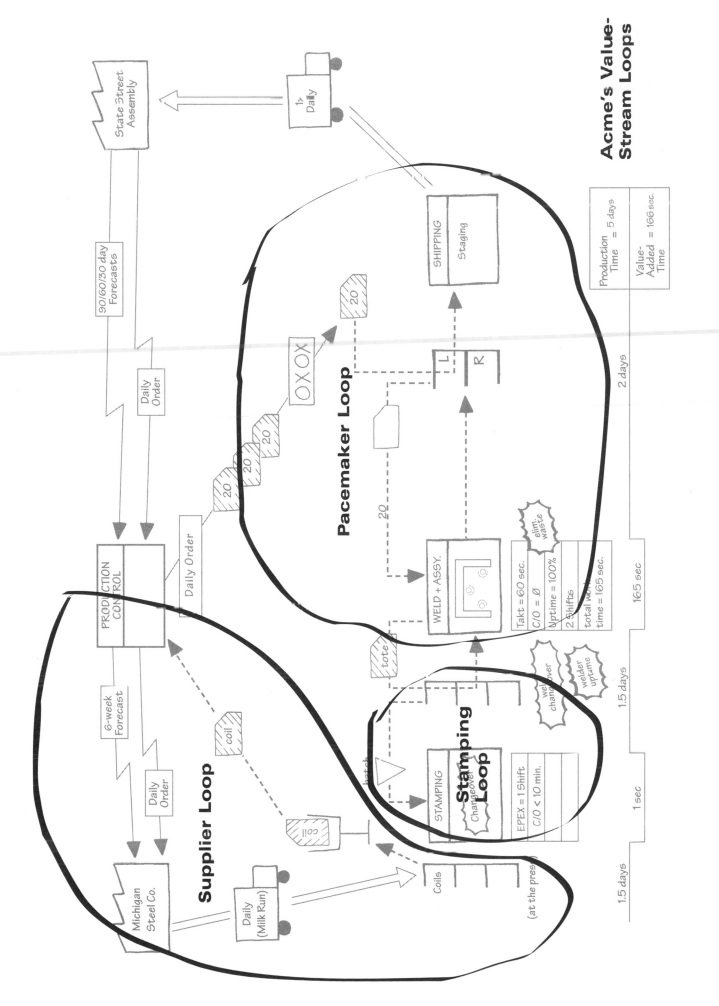

Acme's Value-Stream Loops

State Street Assembly

90/60/30 day Forecasts

Daily Order

1× Daily

PRODUCTION CONTROL

Daily Order

Pacemaker Loop

SHIPPING
Staging

OXOX

20

20 20 20

20

WELD + ASSY.

Takt = 60 sec.
C/O = ∅
Uptime = 100%
2 Shifts
total work time = 165 sec.

elim. waste

L
R

tote

6-week Forecast

Daily Order

coil

Supplier Loop

welder changeover

welder uptime

Stamping Loop

STAMPING
Changeover

EPEX = 1 Shift
C/O < 10 min.

batch

coil

Michigan Steel Co.

Daily (Milk Run)

Coils

(at the press)

Production Time = 5 days

Value-Added = 166 sec.
Time

2 days

165 sec

1.5 days

1 sec

1.5 days

The Value-Stream Plan

Your future-state map shows where you want to go. Now you need to create one more sheet: a yearly value-stream plan. This plan shows:

- exactly what you plan to do by when, step-by-step;
- measurable goals;
- clear checkpoints with real deadlines and named reviewer(s).

The first question that usually arises in planning implementation is, "In what order should we implement?" or "Where do we start?" We suggest you answer these questions by considering the loops in your future-state value stream.

To pick a starting point you can look for loops:

- where the process is well-understood by your people;
- where the likelihood of success is high (to build momentum);
- where you can predict big bang for the buck (but beware, this sometimes leads you to areas that have many major problems to be solved, which can lead to conflicts with the previous criteria).

If you have highlighted the loops on your future-state map, you can number them in order of your implementation plan (use a pencil, because plans do change!) One effective strategy is to begin implementation in your downstream "pacemaker" loop and transition upstream as necessary. The pacemaker loop, being closest to the final customer, acts as the internal "customer" and controls demand in upstream loops. As the flow in the pacemaker becomes lean and consistent it will reveal upstream problems that need attention. However, the "moving upstream" strategy does not preclude simultaneously implementing your future-state objectives in more than one loop of the value stream. For example, we have frequently opted to begin working on batch-size reduction and pull in an upstream fabrication loop while we are still fine-tuning continuous flow and introducing leveling in the downstream pacemaker loop.

Within a value-stream loop, a sequence that your value-stream improvements may generally follow is one that mirrors the key questions for future-state design listed on page 58.

Specifically, improvements to a loop often follow this pattern:

1. Develop a continuous flow that operates based on takt time.
2. Establish a pull system to control production.
3. Introduce leveling.
4. Practice kaizen to continually eliminate waste, reduce batch sizes, shrink supermarkets, and extend the range of continuous flow.

Naturally you'll find that this sequence will vary from case to case and the distinction between the steps may blur to the degree that they are really happening at the same time. Even so, it is beneficial for you to have this general sequential model in your mind as you proceed, recognizing that these implementation objectives are building on each other.

Why the implementation sequence listed above? First, continuous flow gives you the biggest bang for the buck in terms of eliminating waste and shortening lead time. It's also the simplest area to begin working on. (Don't set up a pull system if you can create continuous flow.)

Continuous flow with minimum waste means eliminating overproduction, which then means that you must (and can) standardize your work elements so that production is consistent and predictable to your takt time. You'll then need pull as a means of giving production instruction to the flow (and to kick off the entire production sequence from the customer in the case of the pacemaker loop). Finally, you'll need leveling to achieve a lean flow anytime you have multiple products, simply because lack of leveling will mean that you are still batching your builds of different products. Even if you produce only one product, you still need to level the production volume.

That leaves the last key question, "What process improvements will be necessary for the value stream to flow as your future-state design specifies?" Successfully developing continuous flow, pull, and leveling will demand varying levels of preparatory work. For example, before you can reach a high degree of levelization you will have to gain the ability to execute quick changeovers. Or, before you can expect your assembly cells to operate effectively at takt time, you will need a high level of first-time-through capability and machine reliability. Or your order-entry process needs to be changed

Here is the source of another potential Catch-22: Which comes first, these preparatory process improvements or introducing continuous flow, pull, and leveling improvements? Certainly, they both need to move hand-in-hand to some degree. However, we have found that when in doubt, move forward on making flow improvements and let those flow improvements drive the implementation of supporting process improvements. Otherwise, you can work forever simply striving — and waiting — to attain a high level of process capability. Pitfall to avoid: Don't get stuck in process improvement!

Once you have a sense for the basic order in which you want to implement the elements of your future-state vision, the value-stream manager needs to write them down as the yearly value-stream plan. The format for the value-stream plan is shown with the Acme Stamping example on the next page. The plan will be familiar to you if you have experience with policy deployment, or it may look like a variation of a Gantt chart.

DATE:	JAN 2, 2003							
FACILITY MANAGER:	Barb Smith							
V.S. MANAGER:	Paul Doe							

Product Family Business Objective	V.S. LOOP	Value-Stream Objective	GOAL (measurable)	2003			
				1	**2**	**3**	**4**
Improve profitability in steering brackets	**1** pace-maker	*continuous flow from weld-assembly	zero wip	→	→		
		*kaizen to 165 sec.	≤ 165s c/t	→	→		
		*eliminate weld c/o	< 30s c/o	→			
		*uptime welder #2	100%	→			
		*finished goods pull	2 days FG + pull schedule			→	→
		*material handler routes					
	2 stamping	*stamping pull	1 day inventory + pull schedule				
		* stamping changeover	batch size 300/160 pcs c/o < 10 min				
	3 supplier	* pull for coils with daily delivery	daily delivery & ≤ 1.5 days of coils at press				

VALUE-STREAM PLAN

MONTHLY SCHEDULE								PERSON IN CHARGE	RELATED INDIVIDUALS & DEPTMTS	REVIEW SCHEDULE	
										REVIEWER	DATE
5	6	7	8	9	10	11	12				

Signatures header: PLANT MANAGER | UNION | ENGINEERING | MAINTENANCE

PRODUCT FAMILY:	Steering Brackets

As you might imagine, the key to making your yearly value-stream plan useful is incorporating it into your normal business process, particularly in the budgeting process. No money approved without a value-stream plan! This will make it easier for both sides—requester and approver—once everyone gets used to using the tool (value-stream mapping in its "communication tool" role).

You can also use the yearly value-stream plan to evaluate manufacturing performance quarterly or monthly as a key method of performance review: "Bring me your future-state value-stream map along with an honest progress evaluation every month." We have included an example value-stream review form on the next page. Prior to a review, the value-stream manager should honestly evaluate each implementation objective as on target (**O**), slightly behind (**▲**), or unsuccessful (**✕**).

The key to effective progress review is to "manage the exceptions". That is, during the review do not focus first on what has been accomplished. Focus instead on the **✕** items and, if enough meeting time remains, the **▲** items. For each of these behind-schedule items the manager should ask the value-stream manager, "What do you need in order to get this item on track?" Then the manager can provide targeted support as required.

The idea behind a value-stream review is something we call "plan-based trial-and-error," which refers to blending two usually opposite thought processes: "planning" and "trial-and-error." "Trial-and-error" indicates acceptance that all will not go according to plan and that, in fact, we can learn useful things from failures. But "plan-based" indicates that the typical laissez-faire, "let's try this next" style of trial-and-error is not acceptable. There must be an effort to strive toward plan accomplishment, even as we recognize that the value-stream plan will change and evolve annually. Deviations from the plan are questioned rigorously and accepted only after trial has shown the plan to be less than optimal. This provides the discipline necessary to achieve improvement.

You may or may not want to incorporate the quarterly value-stream review into your personnel appraisal process. The plus of incorporating it includes the facts that it is: 1) a good tool for evaluating performance; and 2) nothing gives teeth to a process more than linking it to appraisals — and therefore paychecks. The negative here, though, is that a key to making the continual current state/future state revision cycle work is ensuring honest, aggressive goal-setting and evaluation. When tied to personnel performance appraisals, future-state plans tend to become less aggressive and progress evaluations more generous.

A final suggestion is to conduct your value-stream reviews on the shop floor while walking the flow.

VALUE STREAM REVIEW

DATE:

FACILITY MANAGER:

V.S MANAGER:

PLANT-LEVEL OBJECTIVE	V.S. LOOP	OBJECTIVE & MEASURABLE GOAL	PROGRESS CONDITIONS	EVALUATION	REMAINING PROBLEMS	POINTS AND IDEAS FOR COMING YEAR'S OBJECTIVES

PRODUCT FAMILY:

◯ = SUCCESS △ = LIMITED SUCCESS ✗ = UNSUCCESSFUL

Value-Stream Improvement is Management's Responsibility

How can we make this work?

As noted earlier in this workbook, value-stream improvement is primarily a management responsibility. Management has to understand that its role is to see the overall flow, develop a vision of an improved, lean flow for the future, and lead its implementation. You can't delegate it. You can ask the front lines to work on eliminating waste, but only management has the perspective to see the total flow as it cuts across departmental and functional boundaries. From our combined experience with many companies in a range of industries over the past fifteen years we can state that the following are needed:

• Constant efforts to eliminate overproduction. If you eliminate overproduction, you will have great flow.

• A firm conviction that lean principles can be adapted to work in your setting, coupled with a willingness to try, fail, and learn.

What you don't often hear about is the process of trial-and-error that Taiichi Ohno went through as he sought to eliminate overproduction at the young Toyota Motor Corporation. Many errors simply go with the territory when implementing change in long-established mass production practices. If you do it right, each approach will be nearer to the target and will add to your understanding. Such reiteration is a normal part of any lean implementation effort and success will be achieved by those who have the determination to personally work through the obstacles.

• Management needs to dedicate time and to really learn this stuff for themselves — learn it to the point that they can actually teach it. And then they need to actually teach it, not primarily in the classroom (although there is a place for that), but in their daily interactions with their staff.

At whatever level, from CEO to plant floor supervisor, the words and deeds of managers must be pushing the creation of a lean value stream. It simply won't work if it's relegated to a few minutes at the weekly staff meeting. It's got to be part and parcel of every day's activities. Practice the mapping concept presented here to the point that it becomes an instinctive means of communication.

• You'll need a way to get people to follow your lead, without always waiting for you to lead them. Begin by focusing your organization on a relatively small number of specific targets (e.g. manage by value-stream maps). You may recognize this process as policy deployment.

Eventually, you should evolve to policy management, which is a much more dynamic process where lower levels of the organization take part in formulating policy as well as carrying it out. As your lean organization matures, you'll find that policy begins to emerge from interaction between levels of the organization, rather than simply emanating from above to be deployed below.

• Close-to-the-operation support, not "self-directed work teams." Close-to-the-operation support means: 1) all "indirect" operations are considered "support" for direct operations; and 2) the work of support operations (production control, supervision, team leaders, material handling, maintenance, problem response) must be tied to the takt and pitch times of the direct value-adding operations.

If we are asking operators to work at takt time, we need to be able to manage within the same takt time framework. For example, ask yourself, "Can my support organization (maintenance, etc.) respond to problems encountered by production operators within takt time?" If the answer is "no" (and it almost always is) then your organization isn't ready for production to operate at takt time.

We are continually amazed at the responses we get when we walk through firms, pick a product at random, and ask the simple question: "Who is responsible for the cost, quality, and on-time delivery of this product from start to finish?"

The usual answer is: "Well, Material Handling is responsible for moving parts between the production steps; the Stamping Department manager is responsible for meeting his schedule; the Welding Department manager is responsible for meeting her schedule; the Shipping Department is responsible for getting the product shipped on time; Production Control is responsible for setting every department's schedule; the Quality Assurance Department head is responsible for insuring that defects are below the maximum acceptable level and..."

In short, no one is responsible.

• Changing the organizational focus from departments to product teams.

• A "value-stream manager" whose job is to lead the people operating the process, not just in manufacturing but in all business functions, and to take responsibility for the cost, quality and delivery of the product in the present state while mapping and leading implementation of the future state.

• Lean manufacturing specialists who can help value-stream managers see waste and introduce the appropriate practices needed to remove its sources.

In the beginning most value-stream managers and their team members will benefit from a bit of technical assistance in sharpening their vision, introducing and refining continuous flow, instituting quick changeover of equipment, installing a pull system, leveling the schedule, and so on. However, the lean specialists must be the coaches rather than the actual implementers, with the clear objective of transferring all of their lean experience to the value-stream manager and others as quickly as possible.

Make sure your lean promotion group is actually on the plant floor, leading the changes, embracing a "hands-on" approach to problem solving, while paying attention to the actual needs of the organization and customer. Also make sure that your lean promotion group helps all business functions, not just manufacturing.

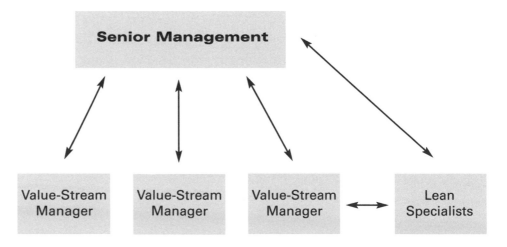

Lean specialists support the implementers and report to senior management.

Note:

The only way we have found to actually learn lean methods is to apply the techniques ourselves hands-on with a bit of coaching. We are certain that this is true for the great majority of managers. The tragedy is that so many managers want to retain a consultant expert to solve their immediate problem for them without need for their active involvement. Of course they discover that they are never able to solve their own problems themselves and often fall into a spiral of consultant dependency. Just say no!

• A new set of performance measures for product teams focused on reducing lead time, space, effort, defects, and missed deliveries, rather than the traditional financial metrics of asset utilization and burden absorption.

Measures should provide meaningful information for managing a lean operation, and must not be counter-productive to lean goals. Unfortunately, our traditional measurement systems do us little good when it comes to trying to manage a lean value stream. After all — remembering that our concern should be improved flow — what impact on flow can we expect from measures that emphasize such things as equipment utilization or labor and overhead? Answer: negative impact!

Unfortunately, few of us are in the position of being able to discard our traditional financial measures (in which— the perfect example of a counter-productive measure — inventory is an asset!). However, what we can do is determine that those measures that provide us with little to no help in running our plants do not interfere with how we manage our plants.

Lean measures for manufacturing performance should adhere to the following principles:

Principle 1: Measures should encourage desired behavior by the front lines.

Principle 2: Measures should provide information for senior managers to make decisions.

Principle 3: Principle 1 takes precedence over Principle 2.

That being said, here is a fine lean-manufacturing measure for any plant: "Is our takt time-based production target achieved every day at the pacemaker process?"

CONCLUSION

Clearly, there is no end to the "future-becomes-present" cycle. This should be the heart of day-to-day management in any organization with a product to sell, whether it be a good, a service, or some combination constituting a solution to the customer's problem. As we've discovered again and again, when you remove sources of waste during a cycle you discover more waste lurking in the next cycle which can be eliminated. The job of lean managers and their teams is keep this virtuous circle going.

This workbook has focused almost entirely on technical aspects of introducing a lean value stream. This is a good place to begin because to be competitive the value stream needs to flow in a way that serves the customer with the overall shortest lead time, lowest cost, highest quality, and most dependable delivery. It shouldn't be sub-optimized to serve the desires of individual processes, departments, functions, or people.

However, making the technical changes will also "pull" the need for change in the people side of the value stream. Adversarial labor/management relations, for example, will hamper implementation efforts and traditional job classifications will not mesh with a truly lean operation. Current ways of measuring performance — led by standard cost accounting — will encourage a regression to mass-production methods. And so on.

Lean value streams must be developed with respect for people. But respect for people should not be confused with "respect for old habits." Developing lean value streams can be hard work, often with one step back for every two forward. Developing a lean value stream exposes sources of waste, which means that people in all business functions may have to change habits. We believe that everyone — management and employees — has a role to play in lean implementation, and that everyone should feel a benefit from it. These benefits can come in many forms: increased competitiveness of the company, a better working environment, greater trust between management and employees, and — not least — a sense of accomplishment in serving your customer.

Whenever there is a product for a customer, there is a value stream. The challenge lies in seeing it. Value-stream maps can be drawn in the same way for practically any business activity and expanded up- and downstream from your company to span from "molecules to customer." We can't provide an example of a value-stream map for every activity here. But we hope *Learning to See* will spur your thinking about your own value streams, and help you introduce lean value streams that fit your industry.

TAKE THE LEAN LEAP

About the Authors

Mike Rother

Mike began his career in the manufacturing division of Thyssen AG and has spent 10 years learning to apply lean practices through consulting at several different companies—both large and small. Mike also teaches at the University of Michigan, Department of Industrial and Operations Engineering, and studies Toyota. He finds there is always another level of lean to practice and understand.

John Shook

John has been learning about lean since 1983 when he joined Toyota to help them transfer its production, engineering, and management systems from Japan to its oversees affiliates and suppliers. Since 1994, he has split his time between directing the University of Michigan, Japan Technology Management Program, serving as senior advisor for the Lean Enterprise Institute, and working with companies and individuals to understand and implement lean manufacturing. And he is ever studying and learning about lean.

Appendix A - Value-Stream Mapping Icons

The icons and symbols for current- and future-state mapping fall into three categories: Material Flow; Information Flow; and General Icons.

Material Icons	Represents	Notes
ASSEMBLY	Manufacturing Process	One process box equals an area of flow. All processes should be labeled. Also used for departments, such as Production Control.
XYZ Corporation	Outside Sources	Used to show customers, suppliers, and outside manufacturing processes.
C/T = 45 sec. / C/O = 30 min / 3 Shifts / 2% Scrap	Data Box	Used to record information concerning a manufacturing process, department, customer, etc.
I — 300 pieces 1 Day	Inventory	Count and time should be noted.
Mon + Wed.	Truck Shipment	Note frequency of shipments.
(striped arrow)	Movement of production material by <u>PUSH</u>	Material that is produced and moved forward before the next process needs it; usually based on a schedule.
(open arrow)	Movement of finished goods to the customer	
(supermarket icon)	Supermarket	A controlled inventory of parts that is used to schedule production at an upstream process.

Material Icons	Represents	Notes
Withdrawal	Withdrawal	Pull of materials, usually from a supermarket.
max. 20 pieces —FIFO→	Transfer of controlled quantities of material between processes in a "First-In-First-Out" sequence.	Indicates a device to limit quantity and ensure FIFO flow of material between processes. Maximum quantity should be noted.

Information Icons	Represents	Notes
←	Manual Information flow	For example: production schedule or shipping schedule.
←	Electronic Information flow	For example via electronic data interchange.
Weekly Schedule	Information	Describes an information flow.
20	Production Kanban (dotted line indicates kanban path)	The "one-per-container" kanban. Card or device that tells a process how many of what can be produced and gives permission to do so.
(hatched box)	Withdrawal Kanban	Card or device that instructs the material handler to get and transfer parts (i.e. from a supermarket to the consuming process).
(triangle)	Signal Kanban	The "one-per-batch" kanban. Signals when a reorder point is reached and another batch needs to be produced. Used where supplying process must produce in batches because changeovers are required.

Information Icons	Represents	Notes
⊙	Sequenced-Pull Ball	Gives instruction to immediately produce a predetermined type and quantity, typically one unit. A pull system for subassembly processes without using a supermarket.
⊻	Kanban Post	Place where kanban are collected and held for conveyance.
◀--▭ --	Kanban Arriving in Batches	
OXOX	Load Leveling	Tool to intercept batches of kanban and level the volume and mix of them over a period of time.
👓	"Go See" Production Scheduling	Adjusting schedules based on checking inventory levels.

General Icons	Represents	Notes
weld changeover / welder uptime	"Kaizen Lightning Burst"	Highlights improvement needs at specific processes that are critical to achieving the value-stream vision. Can be used to plan kaizen workshops.
▯	Buffer or Safety Stock	"Buffer" or "Safety Stock" must be noted.
‿O	Operator	Represents a person viewed from above.

Appendix B: TWI Industries Current State

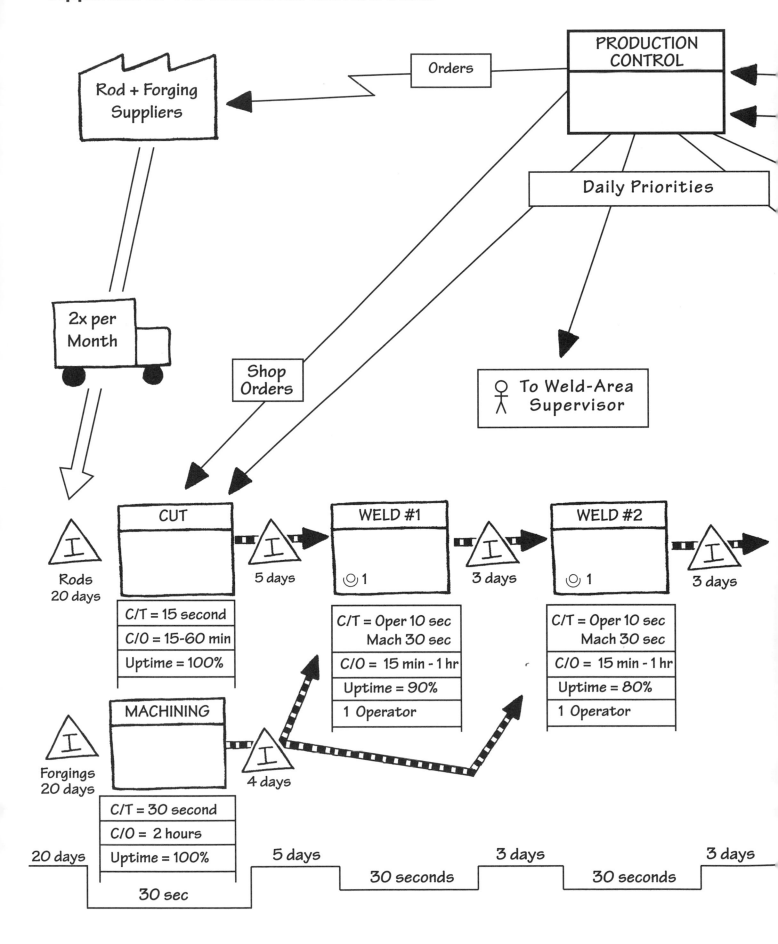

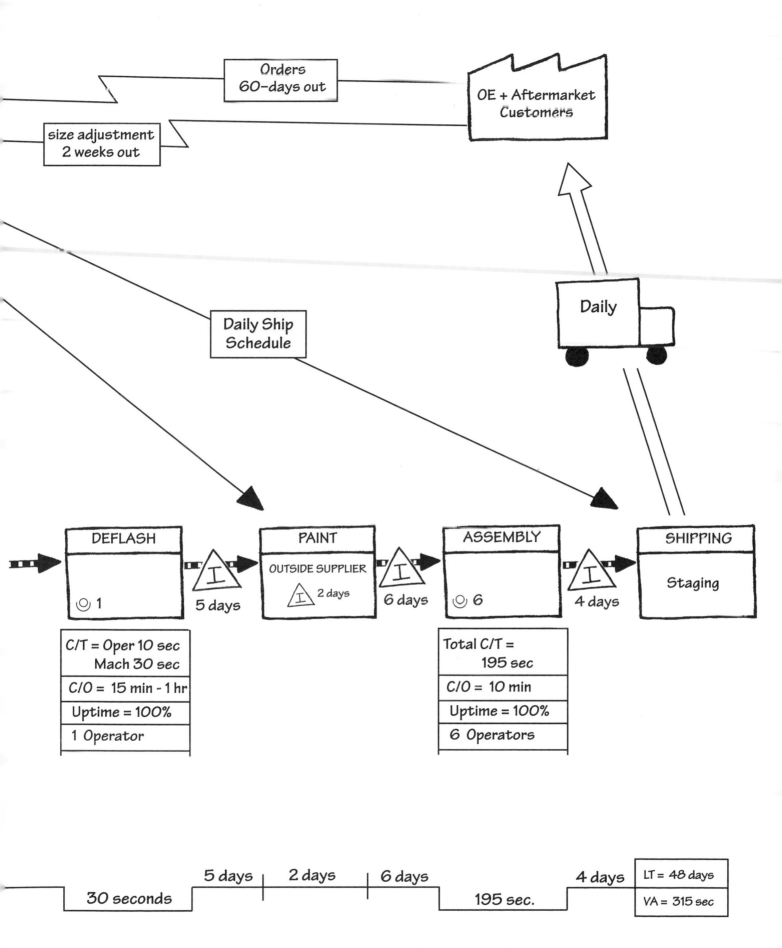

APPENDIX B: TWI INDUSTRIES CURRENT STATE

Appendix C: TWI Industries Future State

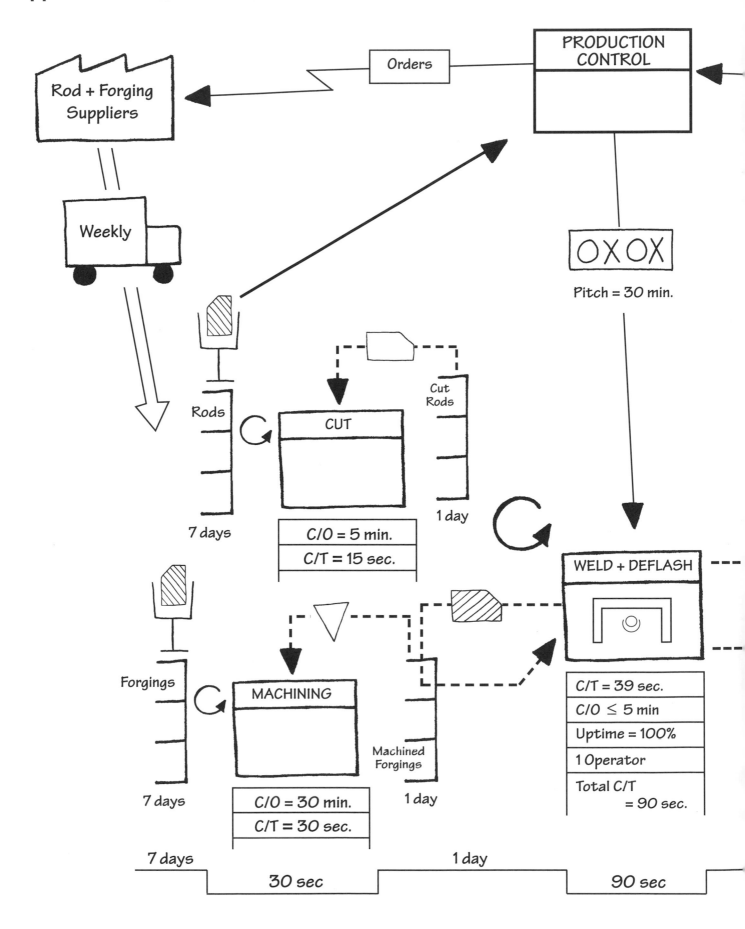

PRODUCTION CONTROL

Orders

Rod + Forging Suppliers

Weekly

OXOX

Pitch = 30 min.

Rods

7 days

CUT

C/O = 5 min.

C/T = 15 sec.

Cut Rods

1 day

Forgings

7 days

MACHINING

C/O = 30 min.

C/T = 30 sec.

Machined Forgings

1 day

WELD + DEFLASH

C/T = 39 sec.

C/O ≤ 5 min

Uptime = 100%

1 Operator

Total C/T = 90 sec.

7 days

30 sec

1 day

90 sec

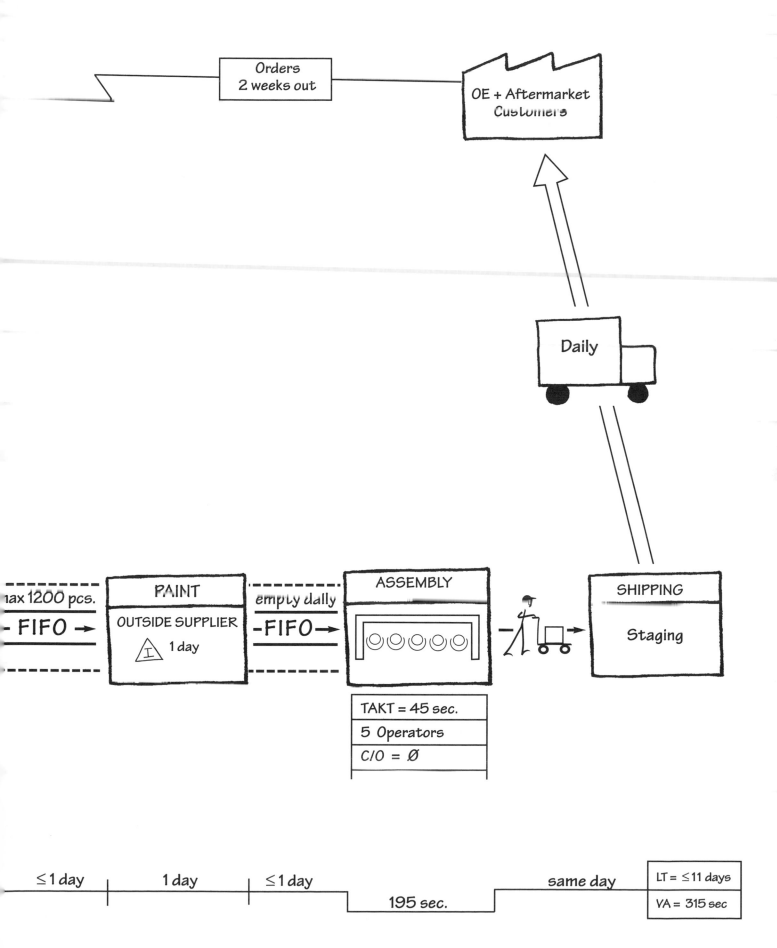

Orders
2 weeks out

OE + Aftermarket
Customers

Daily

max 1200 pcs.

FIFO →

PAINT

OUTSIDE SUPPLIER

⚠ 1 day

empty daily

FIFO →

ASSEMBLY

◎◎◎◎◎

TAKT = 45 sec.

5 Operators

C/O = ∅

SHIPPING

Staging

≤ 1 day   1 day   ≤ 1 day   same day

195 sec.

LT = ≤ 11 days

VA = 315 sec

APPENDIX C: TWI INDUSTRIES FUTURE STATE

Comments to the TWI Industries Future-State Map

TWI's shop floor is swamped with orders that were released too soon and are shuffled and reshuffled to optimize changeovers and meet the most urgent customer requirements. Instead of releasing so many orders to the shop floor, if TWI were to send only 30 minutes of work (one pitch) at a time to the the first welding operation and flow it in FIFO order (first in, first out) from there through shipping, the lead time for producing a customer order could be reduced to under three days (with the middle of those days being at the outside paint supplier). This requires reduction of changeover time in the welding and deflash operations to five minutes or less so that different configuration steering arms could be produced nearer to the sequence in which the customer orders them.

Because customer configuration requirements for tractor steering arms vary so widely from order to order—nearly to the point of being custom products—and the lead time to replenish an order is still quite long, TWI decided that it would be impractical to hold finished steering arms in a supermarket at the downstream end of its value stream. So TWI will need to schedule further upstream, in this case at the first welding operation where product variation arises, and thus have to employ a FIFO flow downstream of that point (see the FIFO lane discussion on page 48). By only releasing 30 minutes worth of work in 30-minute increments at this scheduling point (the "pacemaker process" - see page 49) and following FIFO procedures, TWI can avoid overproduction and "push" in this long FIFO flow.

TWI can develop continuous flow through the weld and deflash operations, which could then be run by one operator who loads and transfers parts from one automatic machine to the next. TWI will need to cycle the weld/deflash flow faster than the takt time of 45 seconds —at approximately 39 seconds—to leave time for 12 changeovers per shift. Because assembly involves no changeover, it can cycle nearer to takt time, which allows assembly to run with five operators.

TWI's 30-minute pitch in this case is based on the 50-piece average order size and the fact that the weld/deflash flow requires a 5-minute changeover between orders. With customer demand of 600 pieces per shift and a cycle time of 39 seconds, there is one hour left over per shift for the 12 changeovers between pitches. To establish the pitch increment, production control will combine small orders and break down large orders in 50-piece increments. Production control will also introduce leveling of the production mix, so that the cut-rod and machined-forging supermarkets upstream can be smaller. So TWI will not produce orders in exactly the sequence as they are received, but very close to it.

With the changes noted above, TWI's customers can now place their orders only two weeks out. Production of cut rods and machined forgings, of which there are fewer varieties than finished steering arms, can be controlled by supermarket pull systems. Likewise, uncut rods and raw forgings can be ordered based on withdrawals out of raw-material supermarkets. This eliminates the need for production control to release orders early to trigger MRP-based raw material orders.

Feedback Form

We've tried to make this workbook easy to use, with simple instructions and clear examples. However, we know from years of experience that applying even the simplest concepts in complex organizations is hard. So we need your help. We provide this simple form for you to help us produce a better *Learning to See*. After you've tried value-stream mapping in your firm, we would greatly appreciate your answering and faxing back to us these three simple questions. As we receive your feedback, we will prepare revisions of the workbook and, through the lean website, notify the lean community of new versions of *Learning to See*.

1. What problems did you encounter in value-stream mapping?

_____

_____

_____

_____

_____

_____

_____

2. What specific changes in *Learning to See* would make the value-stream mapping tool and this workbook more useful?

_____

_____

_____

_____

_____

_____

_____

3. What applications of value-stream mapping have you made outside of discrete parts manufacturing (for example, in raw materials production, process industries, distribution, and services) that you would be willing to share with members of the lean network?

_____

_____

_____

_____

_____

_____

_____

Please fax this form to: Lean Enterprise Institute 617-871-2999
Mail it to: LEI, One Cambridge Center, Cambridge, MA 02142 USA
Or contact us at: www.lean.org